KNO

Many fish are ve_____ only when they are t_____ own kind. If a normally_____ an aquarium with no other members of its family it will feel stressed and unprotected and will also become bored. In an effort to create a little excitement, the fish may even attack every other fish that comes near it.

Solitary fish
Other species are either complete loners or naturally travel in single breeding pairs. Adult cichlid pairs become very territorial and will not tolerate other fish nearby. An even more extreme example— a male Siamese fighting fish cannot be kept in the same tank with another male of its kind or the two will fight to the death.

Shy, nocturnal fish
Sometimes a beginning aquarist will think that something is wrong with a fish that hides behind a rock or half buries itself in the sand all the time, but several species of popular aquarium fish are naturally very timid and shy, active only at dusk or during the night. Some people who keep nocturnal fish light their aquariums very softly so that the fish will be fooled into coming out.

Also by Elizabeth Randolph:

THE
BASIC BOOK
OF
FISH KEEPING

Elizabeth Randolph

FAWCETT CREST • NEW YORK

A Fawcett Crest Book
Published by Ballantine Books
Copyright © 1990 by Elizabeth Randolph

Library of Congress Catalog Card Number: 90-93287

ISBN 0-449-21776-0

Manufactured in the United States of America

First Edition: January 1991

CONTENTS

Contents

Contents

Contents

ACKNOWLEDGMENTS

Special thanks to the following people for their time, help, and expertise: Daniel F. Bebak, Curator, Mote Marine Science Aquarium, Sarasota, Florida; Dr. Paul V. Loiselle, Assistant Curator, Freshwater Fishes, New York Aquarium; Brian Morris of Clearwater, Florida; Ken Strassfield, owner of "Pets Ahoy" in Norwalk, Connecticut; and Dr. Michael K. Stoskopf, Professor and Head of Companion Animal and Special Species Medicine at the College of Veterinary Medicine, North Carolina State University in Raleigh, North Carolina.

Thanks also to my always encouraging editor, Barbara Dicks, and to my patient, understanding and always helpful and supportive husband, Arthur Hettich.

ELIZABETH RANDOLPH

INTRODUCTION

Fish keeping as a hobby has grown by leaps and bounds in the last few years. It is now the second most popular hobby in the United States, topped only by photography. It is estimated that hundreds of millions of dollars are spent on tropical fish and goldfish each year in this country, and at least an equivalent amount of money goes toward equipment, supplies, and food for pet fish.

Fish make ideal pets in our increasingly busy, urbanized society. Unlike cats, dogs, or even birds, they are quiet, take up very little space, don't give people allergies, don't need to be walked or exercised, don't get lonely if you can't give them a lot of attention, don't become stressed and soil the carpet or tear up the furniture if you leave them alone for the weekend, and generally represent a relatively small initial investment and ongoing maintenance expense.

At the same time, fish are enjoyable and interesting to keep. Individual fish actually become quite tame and responsive. Their owners get to know them well and become attached to them and vice versa. Other fish owners go beyond simple enjoyment and become involved in serious breeding and even in fish shows.

It is well known that studies at the University of Pennsylvania and elsewhere have demonstrated that fish-watching has a calming effect on people and can lower blood pressure in both healthy people and those with hypertension.

However, as Dr. Michael Stoskopf, former chief of medicine at the National Aquarium in Baltimore,[*] pointed out in a recent talk, "The tranquility induced by watching an aquarium is rapidly diminished when the inhabitants are sick or dying, and the little bodies that you care about are not swimming around happily but are floating on the surface of the water." According to Dr. Stoskopf, the number one reason that people stop keeping fish is that they can't keep them alive. Far from being calming and beneficial, fish keeping can be a very frustrating experience, if you have to start over with new fish continuously.

How can you avoid this pitfall? Do as much research as possible *before* putting any fish into an aquarium. Before you start, however, you should be aware that modern fish keeping is an inexact science. It's well known in fish-keeping circles that if you ask ten experienced people about a specific aspect of fish care, you'll probably get ten different answers, all of which may be equally good ones. There are so many variables among different kinds of fish, different individual fish, different combinations of fish, different factors that will affect water chemistry and the balance of a fish tank, and so forth, that every successful fish keeper may have had a slightly different experience.

But there are some broad, general aspects of successful fish keeping that all of the experts agree on. They are: an intelligent, informed choice of fish and equipment, careful attention to the maintenance of a healthy environment, the ability to recognize trouble before it becomes serious and the knowledge to cope with it as best you can in order to keep your fish healthy and content.

These are the topics dealt with in this book.

---

[*] See page 243 for current biographical information.

PART ONE

Under-standing Fish

The Physical Fish

Before you can have any real success keeping fish, you need a basic understanding of what makes these interesting creatures work.

There are over 20,000 known species of fish in the world today, with more being discovered by scientists in remote areas of the earth. With this many species, it is not strange that there are many physical and behavioral differences in fish.

Common Characteristics

All fish are vertebrates. That is, they have a spinal column. They are the oldest known vertebrates, ancestors of all other vertebrates on earth, including Man. The evolution of fish to amphibians, reptiles, birds, and then to mammals is well documented. Their many forms and species have developed and become adapted to various kinds of water habitats.

Despite the differences necessitated by habitat—such as

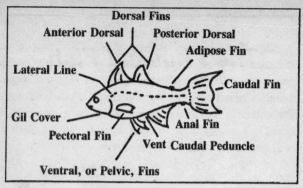

The External Fish

the kind and depth of water, currents and temperature, underwater topography, plant life, and availability of food—there are some general characteristics that are possessed by all species of fish.

Almost all species have become adapted to living exclusively in water. (Although there are a few fish that can breathe air, they will *not* be included in this book.) A fish obtains oxygen and necessary minerals from water which is taken in through its gills (more about this process under *Respiration,* see *page 12.*) It must have the proper balance of oxygen and the proper minerals in the water it lives in to survive.

Like reptiles, all fish are cold-blooded. That means that they cannot regulate their own body temperatures as mammals can. A fish's internal body temperature is always the same as that of the medium—water—around it. But, unlike most reptiles which are amphibious, a fish cannot climb out of water that is too chilly and bask in the sun to warm up. A fish in an aquarium is virtually a prisoner—totally dependent on the "keeper" to maintain properly balanced water at the right temperature.

The External Fish

Although all fish are made up of basically the same parts, they may differ greatly in external appearance. Color, body shape, fin and mouth placement, and tail size and shape all reflect adaptations made by a particular type of fish to its environment. Even the most uninformed observer can quickly learn to notice certain salient characteristics that will identify a particular type of fish.

BODY SHAPE

Most fish bodies are bilaterally symmetrical—that is, both sides are alike. Traditionally, a fish's body is a streamlined, torpedo (fusiform) shape, tapering gently outward from the mouth to the midsection, and then gradually tapering down to meet the joining of the tail. This shape, along with fins that can be easily folded flat against the body, forms a smooth, nonresistant package that can glide quickly and easily through the water. Torpedo-shaped fish are very fast swimmers. They are good at catching food and escaping from predators.

Slight adaptations in this torpedo shape can be seen in some fish. A fish with a flat-bottomed body, such as a catfish, is able to stay on the bottom and feed, while one with a straight, flat back is adapted to swimming near the top of the water without breaking the surface. Even more extreme in variation, some fish, such as the triangular-shaped hatchetfish, have flat backs and extremely well-developed body muscles that enable it to skim just below (and sometimes above) the water's surface.

Fish that have other body shapes cannot swim as quickly as the torpedo-shaped species, but they have adapted to their habitats and developed other ways of protecting themselves against predators. Laterally compressed, thin-bodied, disc-shaped fish such as some of the cichlid family—angelfish and discus fish, for example—are adept at slipping in between the clumps of weeds and grasses that are found in the shallow river edges they inhabit for cover. Disc-shaped saltwater fish use the cracks in coral for protection.

Bottom-living fish with flat, depressed pancakelike body forms, such as flounders, are usually found in ocean waters, and can readily hide themselves beneath sandy bottoms.

Streamer-type fish with long cylindrical bodies are able to slither through the rushes and reeds found in rivers and lakes with muddy bottoms, and can easily hide in small holes in rocks. Eels and pipefish fall into this category.

The most obvious outward form of protection is that of the armored fish, such as some catfish and slow-moving marine boxfishes and spiny brackish or freshwater puffer-fish.

FINS

Most fish have seven fins, two pairs and three single, midline fins. These fins can be very different in size and placement and are supported by rays that are either hard and spiny or soft. Spiny-rayed fins are generally in one piece, while soft-rayed fins are separated or branched. Fins serve to balance, steer, and propel a fish through water and can be raised and lowered by special small muscles.

The tail, or caudal fin, varies considerably in different fish species. It acts as a rudder and, along with the accompanying wavelike motion of the fish's body, helps to give the final push to propel it through the water. Most fast-swimming fish have large forked or crescent-shaped tails. In some species, males have an extended caudal fin. This long, pointed extension, seen in swordtails, seems to be merely ornamental. Extra long, lacy caudal fins have been carefully developed through aquarium-breeding in some species such as fancy goldfish and Siamese fighting fish. These fish are usually slow swimmers. The area where a fish's body narrows to join the tail (sometimes referred to as the tail stalk) is called the caudal peduncle.

A fish's dorsal fin is in the center of the back and acts as a stabilizer, keeping the fish upright in the water. It is often carried erect, like a sail, and can convey aggression or serve to attract a female. Sometimes, it is modified to become a defensive weapon. The lionfish's dorsal fin, for example, has long, hollow spines that contain venom. Dorsal fins vary a great deal in size and shape and may be single, divided into anterior (front) and posterior (rear) fins, or in some cases into several small fins. In some species, such as characins, there is also a small, fleshy, rayless fin called an adipose fin located on the back near the tail.

The other single fin is the anal fin, located on the underside of a fish, behind the vent. It can be long or fin-shaped and act as a rudder, or it may help to propel a fish through water. In the case of livebearing fish, the male's anal fin has modified rays and is a tubelike organ that helps direct sperm into the female's vent during spawning. Some males in the characin family have tiny barbs or hooks on their anal fins that enable them to hold the female close while spawning.

There are two sets of paired fins, the pectoral fins, located just behind the gills, and the pelvic, or ventral, fins, which are beneath the midsection of the fish in front of the anal fin. Both of these pairs of fins help a fish to steer and stabilize itself while moving in the water. Pectoral fins are often seen moving very quickly in a rotating fashion, just like oars or paddles, helping a fish to change direction or turn in the water. They also serve as brakes when held at right angles to the body. It is these fins that evolved into flippers and then legs, enabling some fish eventually to become amphibians. Some fish, like hatchetfish, have large winglike pectorals that help them to glide through the air.

Pelvic fins have sometimes been referred to as the "hind legs" of fish. Catfish females use their pelvic fins to carry fertilized eggs, while freshwater angelfish have well-developed pelvic fins that can be used as defensive weapons. In some species, the pelvic fins also serve as sensory organs and help to locate food.

SKIN, SCALES, AND COLOR

The thick, tough inner layer (dermis) of a fish's skin covers the entire body, including the eyes, and contains color pigments. It also houses various nerves which act as sensory receptors (see *Lateral Line, page 14*), and is usually covered by a thinner outer layer of skin called the epidermis. The barbels (long, fleshy, whiskerlike "feelers" attached to their mouths) of catfish, barbs, and loaches originate in the skin.

The scales seen on most aquarium fish except Catfish originate in the thick inner skin. There are several types of scales, which overlap to form a streamlined, protective body coating. The skin also contains mucus, or slime, glands that produce a thin, slippery, parasite-repelling layer that coats the scales. In the cichlid family, this mucus also serves as food for newly hatched fry.

Fish can control the shade or intensity of color that they display. Color can be used to camouflage a fish by allowing it to blend in with its surroundings or to confuse by means of disruptive coloration to conceal the fish's body shape. Fear, ill health, or simply a general unhappiness with the surroundings can cause a usually brilliantly colored fish to become pale. Some fish, such as pencilfish, normally change color at night, when it becomes dark. Color is also used to identify a fish to other fish and to attract a mate. Many male fish become intensely colored during the mating season, and some females have high color after breeding so that their fry can easily see and identify them.

There are two kinds of color-producing cells in a fish's skin: chromatophores and iridocytes. Chromatophores contain granules of pigment, while iridocytes reflect light and colors outside the fish, producing the familiar silvery-white iridescence seen on most fish. It is the chromatophores that can change a fish's hue. The intensity of color produced by the chromatophores is controlled by a fish's reaction to its environment.

MOUTH

Most fish have mouths that seem big in comparison with their body size. The shape and position of a fish's mouth is a good indicator of its diet and mode of eating.

Some fish have teeth in their mouths to help them in grasping and tearing food. Others have no teeth in their mouths, but do have bony plates (or extra teeth) in their pharynxes to break food down.

Bottom-feeding fish that suck in their food, like most loaches, usually have underslung mouths with elongated upper lips, with the opening located underneath their bodies. Their mouths are often fringed with barbels that help them locate food. Midwater algae-grazers also may have barbels attached to underslung mouths.

A surface-feeder's mouth is located at the top of the head and is upturned. There is a shovellike bottom lip so that the fish can scoop up insects that are floating on the top of the water.

Fish that swim and eat in the middle part of the water usually have straight mouths placed at the tip of the snout,

Mouth Shapes and Positions

Surface-feeders have upturned mouths that enable them to capture floating insects.

Midwater-feeders' mouths are usually straight and located in the center of the snout so that they can grab food as it floats by.

Bottom-feeders and algae-grazers have downturned mouths located on the underside of their heads. They usually are equipped with sensitive barbels that help them to locate food.

enabling them to grab food as it floats by. As mentioned above, some midwater fish that eat algae have underslung mouths that aid them in gathering algae from flat surfaces.

The Internal Fish

Every fish has a complex nervous system, a heart, liver, kidneys, stomach, reproductive organs, and intestines. Many of these organs and systems work in the same way as those of other animals, but fish do have a few special characteristics that enable them to survive in their watery environment.

DIGESTIVE WASTE

The digestive system of fish differs greatly according to diet, and there is still a lot about the way fish digest and utilize their food that is not fully known. Most digestive wastes are disposed of out of the vent, which is located just in front of the anal fin. The vent is the opening for an internal cavity called the cloaca, into which intestinal, urinary, and genital tracts all open.

In addition, some fish deposit waste products just underneath their own skin. These wastes, known as guanin, make up the iridocytes that reflect light (see *Color, page 8*).

BODY FLUIDS

Because fish are surrounded by water, a process known as *osmosis* has a direct effect on their bodies. Osmosis is a phenomenon in which water seeks to equalize its density and will travel through a permeable or semipermeable membrane from a solution that is less concentrated to one that is more highly concentrated.

Some fish membranes are permeable and allow water and some salts to go through them. Thus, because of osmosis, a freshwater fish, whose blood contains a higher concentration of salts than the water surrounding it, is in constant danger of swelling up and bursting. It is a semipermeable bag of saltwater stuck in a big pot of fresh water, and the water is constantly coming into its body through the gills and all of the membranes in the fish's intestine. So, the fish must continuously pump large amounts of fluids out of its body through urine and its gills. Naturally, freshwater fish drink very little, if any, water.

Saltwater fish, on the other hand, are in constant danger of drying out because their bodies contain less salt than the water surrounding them and they are constantly losing fluids. A marine fish is like a dilute bag stuck in a big pot of saltwater. Therefore, it needs to drink a lot of water, urinate little, and excrete excess salt in an effort to maintain its body fluid levels.

The process by which a fish compensates for the excess or lack of fluid in its body due to osmosis is known as "osmoregulation." If a fish's scales are damaged in any way it will allow more fluids to leave or enter its body and this delicate balance will be affected.

RESPIRATION

Fish take in water through their mouths and pass it out through their gills. The exchange of gasses takes place in a fish's gills, which extract oxygen from the water. The oxygen is then circulated through a fish's body in its bloodstream. Some fish are able to rise to the surface of the water and gulp air which is then processed in a special pouchlike organ. Fish with suckermouths, such as catfish and loaches, have divided gills or extra gill slits so that they can take in water while still sucking food in with their mouths.

Since water contains less available oxygen than air, and the warmer the water the less oxygen in solution, tropical fish must process a great deal of water in order to obtain enough oxygen. Ammonia, a waste product of a fish's metabolism, is passed out from a fish's gills along with carbon dioxide. This ammonia must be removed from the water because bacterial action will change it into poisonous nitrates; more about this in *Chapter Nine*.

SWIM-BLADDERS (GAS BLADDERS)

Almost all aquarium fish except for some bottom-dwellers have a gas bladder, or swim-bladder, that expands and contracts in response to the pressure of the water outside of the fish and allows it to maintain its equilibrium and stay at any level in the water that it desires. The gas is secreted from nearby blood vessels, and reabsorbed by a different set of blood vessels. Some fish fill their swim-bladders with air that they gulp at the water's surface. In some cases, the swim-bladder is linked by small bones to the inner ear and acts as a sound amplifier. These bones are called the Weberian ossicles.

Fish Senses

Like all living creatures, fish have an elaborate sensory system that enables them to capture messages from their environment and send them to their brain via nervous impulses, where they are interpreted and then acted on.

VISION

Fish usually have large eyes with no eyelids. The lenses are big, thick, and round in order to capture as much light as possible, because light does not travel far in water. In most aquarium species, the eyes are located on the sides of the head. This means that fish have monocular peripheral vision. That is, they can see in all directions on both sides of their bodies, but lack binocular vision or depth perception. In most instances, each eye can move independently, which adds to the range of the fish's vision.

Although their vision is acute and they can see light and motion well, most fish cannot focus clearly on objects that are more than about two feet away. Interestingly, their lenses do not change shape in order to focus an image on the retinal surface; instead the entire lens moves in and out. All but deep-sea fishes are able to perceive colors.

SMELL

Two or more nostrils are located just above a fish's mouth. They are not used for breathing, but are directly connected to a smell organ. Fish have a keen sense of smell which they use primarily to locate food but it also helps them to find other fish while schooling and to recognize familiar locations.

HEARING

Fish have no visible outer ears. Their inner ears are divided into two parts that control equilibrium and hearing. Unlike light, sound travels far in water and is very easily detected by fish. Fish are extremely sensitive to vibrations in the water, due to their good hearing and to their lateral-line sense organ (*see below*). As mentioned, some species have particularly acute hearing due to the amplification of sound in their swim-bladders.

LATERAL LINES

Fish have additional sense organs, called lateral lines. In most aquarium fish, these lines, or nerve- and fluid-filled canals, can be seen extending along each side of a fish's body, from just behind the gills to the caudal peduncle. They look like a raised welt that might have been made by scratching the fish's skin with a fingernail. In some fish, they are branched or curved, and may even extend to the snout.

With the aid of this system, fish can detect water currents, vibrations, and soundwaves, enabling them to navigate and to locate other members of their species in the murkiest of waters. It is thought that these vibrations are amplified in the swim-bladders of some species. Blind fish are able to swim through the most complicated mazes by means of this sensory system.

ELECTRICITY

To a greater or lesser extent, all fish can generate and discharge electricity. Some, like electric eels, rays, and catfish, are able to give severe shocks, which are used as a protective mechanism and to stun prey. Most fish, however, simply emit low-voltage currents that form an electrical field around their bodies. When this field is broken it alerts a fish to the presence of obstacles or other fishes in the immediate vicinity.

2

Fish Behavior

Many neophyte fish keepers are very surprised when their charges do more than simply swim around in the tank looking pretty. Like all creatures, fish are living, breathing, and feeling animals. And, just as all animals do, individual fish have personalities. As Dr. Michael Stoskopf, former Chief of Medicine at the National Aquarium in Baltimore, remarked, "If a person can be said to have a personality like a fish, then it stands to reason that fish must have personalities."

It has been scientifically proven that the fish brain has the capacity of learning by association and most fish learn very quickly to respond to the people who feed them. A fish often clearly displays very definite likes and dislikes, swimming up to the water's surface to greet one person, while ignoring another's presence. An individual fish may sometimes also seem to loathe another fish in a tank, constantly chasing it and picking on it for no apparent reason.

It is important for a potential fish owner to understand the normal behavior of the fish that he intends to put together in a tank. Some kinds of fish will not mix well—an extremely timid, slow-moving fish, for instance, will suffer if put in the same tank with a number of aggressive, fast-swimming individuals. Certain species of fish naturally occupy different levels of water, and it is important to stock a tank with this in mind so that the inhabitants can co-exist peacefully without constantly getting in each other's way and stealing each other's food. Although these may seem to be common-sense "rules," they can be easy to overlook when a particular fish seems especially interesting or desirable.

A lot can be learned about normal fish behavior simply by observation and conversation with knowledgeable people. But it can help to be aware of some common fish behavior patterns.

Emotional Stress

Fear, aggression, anger, boredom, territorial guarding, and sexual drive can all affect an individual fish's behavior and may cause it to become stressed.

A fish in a tank is in an unnatural situation. No matter how large the aquarium may be, a fish in it is a prisoner of its environment. Unlike a free-swimming fish in a natural setting, an aquarium fish that finds itself in an unpleasant or threatening situation cannot simply leave to find more space or to get away from an individual that is bothering it.

By observing the normal everyday behavior of the fish in an aquarium, a fish keeper will get to know their habits and idiosyncrasies. Learning how a fish usually acts can help the keeper recognize behavioral changes that might signify a problem.

Just as stress has a physiological effect on other animals, fish can be badly affected if they are constantly under pressure because of environmental conditions. A fish that is stressed is always more susceptible to disease. More about behavioral changes that indicate physical problems and disease are in *Chapter Twelve*.

A fish that constantly feels crowded and harassed by the other fish in the tank, for instance, may spend all of its time trying to get away, racing around the tank heedlessly, bumping into things and even injuring itself. This individual may become so stressed that it will eventually sicken and die. While a fish that is actually being picked on may have to hide to avoid attack, one that continuously feels the need to guard its territory may spend all of its time chasing and fighting with tank-mates. In both cases, the individual may be so preoccupied with either escape or attack that it doesn't have time to eat.

Overcrowding and the wrong combination of fish in a tank are usually the underlying causes of obvious, severe stress in one or more fish. Usually the best course for a fish keeper is to change the number and combination of fish in the tank. The ideal solution may be to begin another tank to house the larger, more aggressive fish, or to simply remove one or more serious offenders from a community tank.

Social Behavior

Just like other animals, some fish are naturally gregarious and others prefer to be alone. Over the years, various types of behavior evolved that were suitable to the environment. Small fish that swim in fairly open waters usually band together in large groups or schools. When hundreds of fish move rapidly together in synchrony as if one individual, it affords each one better protection against a predator, which will find it hard to single out just one fish for dinner. Fish that live in areas where there is a lot of natural vegetation, on the other hand, are better off living singly or in pairs so that they can quickly dart between grasses and reeds for cover. These more solitary fish tend to swim more slowly than those that travel in schools. There are many other factors that influence whether or not a given family of fish prefers to live in a large group of its kind or not, but this preference is a basic part of every individual fish's behavior.

GREGARIOUS FISH

Many fish are very gregarious and are happy only when they are together with several of their own kind. These are usually referred to as schooling, or shoaling, fish and they constantly swim rapidly in evenly spaced tandem with members of their own family. Some popular aquarium fish that are schooling fish are the tetras, danios, barbs, and mollies.

If a normally gregarious fish is kept alone in an aquarium with no other members of its family it will feel stressed and unprotected and will also become bored. A bored fish may act in a couple of ways. It may sulk, become inactive, and lose interest in the world around it, including food. Such an individual will not survive for long. Or it may become excessively aggressive toward other fish in the tank. In an effort to create a little excitement, the fish may attack every other fish that comes near it—chasing and nipping other fish relentlessly.

It is important to be sure that your gregarious fish has several other members of its own family in the tank with it as companions to keep it company and to prevent it from becoming bored.

SOLITARY FISHES

Other species of fish are either complete loners or naturally travel in single breeding pairs. Cichlids, for instance, school when young but once they have matured they break off from the group into pairs. Adult cichlid pairs become very territorial and will not tolerate other fish nearby, especially other species, and should be kept in a single-species tank. An even more extreme example: a male Siamese fighting fish, or betta, cannot be kept in the same tank with another male of its kind or the two will fight to the death. Bettas, however, are peaceful with fish of other species.

Many other fish are quite territorial and quarrelsome with their own species once they reach adulthood, and it is best to keep just one individual or a single pair in a tank.

An interesting device used by experienced aquarists to keep excessively territorial, aggressive, mating fish such as cichlids from attacking each other is to provide some diversion in the form of "dither" fish. Peaceful, very active, quick-moving schooling fish such as zebra danios, for instance, are perfect in the role of "dither" fish. In the continuous, rapid journeys from one end of the tank to the other, they will regularly intrude into the cichlid's territory and distract it from a quarrel with another cichlid. The slower-moving, larger fish will chase the smaller invaders who will simply scoot away without harm, only to return moments later.

SHY, NOCTURNAL FISH

Sometimes a beginning aquarist will think that something is wrong with a fish that hides behind a rock or half buries itself in the sand all of the time, but there are several species of popular aquarium fish that are naturally very timid and shy. These fish are usually nocturnal, active only at dusk or during the night when no one else is stirring. They can sometimes be seen in the daytime if their keepers are very clever at luring them out with especially delicious food. Some people who keep nocturnal fish light their aquariums very softly so that the fish will be fooled into coming out. Bottom-dwellers, such as most loaches and several varieties of catfish are especially shy and nocturnal.

It is very important to provide plenty of hiding places for these shy fish so that they can always find cover. Without a safe place to hide, a timid fish will become very stressed and probably won't survive.

Communication

It is obvious that fish are able to communicate with each other, especially within their own families or species. They use all of the senses described in the preceding chapter in order to signal to each other and interpret those signals.

CHEMICAL AND ELECTRICAL COMMUNICATION

Although little is actually known about some of these subtle means of communication, we do know that fish are able to send signals to each other that are interpreted by smell and by taste. Some schooling fish, for example, give off a very specific odor if their scales are damaged by a predator. This odor warns other members of the school of danger. Because some species, such as those with barbels, have more highly developed senses of smell than others, it is assumed by scientists that they may use their keen olfactory organs in ways beside food-gathering aids.

Fish that are able to emit electrical shocks may use these impulses to attract the opposite sex as well as for protection and food-gathering.

COLOR CHANGING

The ability of fish to change color serves several purposes. Each species developed certain colors that suited the environment and provided optimum camouflage. Bottom-dwellers in particular are often able to change their color very quickly as they travel from one surface to another. The iridescent, silvery bellies of most fish provide perfect protection from a hunter swimming beneath them, by blending in with the surrounding water. From the standpoint of a hungry bird swimming above the water, the dark line along the top of the spine of most fish makes them less visible. A fish that senses danger or is afraid will often lose its bright hues and turn either dark or quite pale in order to better disguise itself. Dark vertical bars on a fish's side can be a sign of fright or of sexual arousal.

Fish may change color for other reasons. Extreme age and illness can cause a fish to change color. Often a stressed fish loses its hue and turns dark. An unhealthy fish may become pale—more about this in *Chapter Twelve*.

But color changes are also used for communication between fish. The males of many species become especially vivid when they want to attract a mate. Female cichlids assume a bright coloration after spawning so that their newborn fry can easily locate them.

BODY AND FIN MOTIONS

Most changes in the posture of a fish's body and fins are used to communicate either aggression or submission.

As we've already mentioned, aggressive behavior can be the result of several different causes. Usually it is territorial in nature, but sometimes aggression in an individual is merely the result of boredom. Overcrowding in a community tank can bring out the worst in even the most mild-mannered fish that feels it must fight in order to maintain enough space. Fighting and aggression over food is, of course, usually not a factor with most well-fed aquarium fishes.

Some fish are territorial all of the time and will guard their particular segment of the tank against all comers. But even the most tolerant, even-tempered fish will usually become territorially aggressive during the breeding season. This is especially true of nonschooling fish that live in pairs.

A fish or pair of fish that are guarding their nest area, eggs, or newly hatched fry will display certain warning signals to an individual that ventures too close. First, one of the adults will place its body in a position that is broadside to the area it is guarding. Its mouth may be open or slightly ajar.

Usually, these motions will be accompanied by a stiffly erected dorsal fin and flaring gill covers. (This is not always an aggressive stance, however. It can also signify sexual excitement and signalling.) In some fish, such as the Siamese fighting fish, all of the fins are stiffened and stand out from the body in a very fierce-looking way. At the same time, the fish's gill covers are opened until they are almost at right angles to its body. This entire action can be compared to piloerection in dogs and cats, where each individual hair stands on end all over the body, and to the puffing-up of the feathers and head crests of birds that want to appear as large and ferocious as possible to their adversaries.

If the invading fish still doesn't go away, the defending fish may engage in tail-beating, moving the tail fin rapidly in the water to make warning waves. Finally, if the fish are of equal size and strength and neither gives way, an actual fight may develop. The fish defending its territory may have to resort to bodily pushing the other fish away, tearing at it, trying to wound it and remove some scales.

The offending fish may be killed, unless it assumes a

23

submissive position, with its fins folded against itself and its entire body hanging vertically and limply in the water. If the offending fish is smaller or slower than the aggressive individual, the aggressor may simply chase it away, nipping at its tail and fins. Sometimes a fish becomes a constant victim, and is chased continually and nipped until its fins become ragged and moth-eaten. This can become a bad habit on the part of the aggressor, and the victim of the chase may hide, become depressed, and stop eating.

Proper tank furnishings can help to avert this kind of trouble. Nooks and crannies will provide a suitable home for a pair of breeding fish, allowing other tank inhabitants to swim freely in other parts of the tank. By the same token, appropriate hiding places will allow a peaceful, quiet fish to get away from it all when necessary.

A fish that is moving its pectoral fins rapidly in a fanning motion may be irrigating its eggs. Body motions are also used by some fish as sexual tools. A male may use his body and tail to push the female of his choice into proper mating position, and a male livebearer will extend his tubelike anal fin toward the female to attract her.

"VOCAL" COMMUNICATION

Although it's now quite well known that humpback whales sing long, complicated songs and that dolphins possess a highly complex language, it never occurs to many people that nonmammal water dwellers like fish can, and do, communicate through sounds. We know that water is a good sound conductor and that most fish have keen hearing, so the concept shouldn't be so strange.

Although it is not yet clear to scientists exactly what the various fish sounds signify, they are probably used to signal position or territory, to attract or repel other fish, and as warning. Underwater microphones—hydrophones—can pick up a cacophony of sounds in the average aquarium. Some aquarists have even connected a hydrophone to a tape recorder to hear what their fish are "saying" when no one's around to bother them.

Aquarium fish have been heard to buzz, click, clack, growl, croak, chirp, and emit a continuous, high-pitched sound. Some rub their teeth, either mouth or pharyngeal, together to make sounds. Others rap or thump various bones against their swim-bladder, which amplifies the sound. Air can be forced through the swim-bladder, producing a barking, or burping, sound. Gill covers and fins are sometimes beaten against the body.

Seahorses click the bones in their necks and some cichlids make a sort of buzzing sound to keep their fry nearby.

Whatever kind of sounds a fish may make, each individual probably has its very own "voice" by which its friends and family are able to recognize it.

Other Behaviors

Some fish naturally engage in unusual body motions. Bottom-sitting, for instance, is normal for many slow-moving algae-eaters like catfish. Some catfish also normally swim upside-down to graze. Air-gulping at the surface is regularly engaged in by Siamese fighting fish, some gouramis, and others. Hatchetfish, pencilfish, and many other small species will jump out of the water, given the opportunity, while others, like the spotted headstander, spend most of their time in an almost vertical position, head-down. As long as an unusual body position or motion is normal for a particular kind of fish, there is no need for concern. It is only when a fish acts in a way that is *not* usual that you need to worry.

SLEEPING

Because fish have no eyelids, people often think that they do not sleep. Fish do, however, sleep or rest. Most are diurnal, awake during the day and sleeping at night. They usually rest quietly either in midwater or on the bottom of the tank. Some may bury themselves partially in the sand or gravel at the bottom of the tank. Dr. Stoskopf tells of several emergency calls he has received in the middle of the night from fish owners who arrived home late, turned on the lights, and found all of their fish lying on the bottom of the tank, apparently either very ill or dead. He sleepily reassured them that they had probably simply interrupted their fish while they were sleeping.

Of course, nocturnal fish engage in just the opposite behavior—they rest all during the day and come out to feed and swim around as soon as the lights dim or go out.

Some saltwater coral fish actually create a sack out of mucus to wrap themselves in while they sleep.

Fish apparently also yawn occasionally.

PLAYING

Some very lively fish engage in what could be interpreted as play behavior. Short, nonaggressive chases are often observed between fish—sometimes the participants take turns being the chaser and "chasee." Sometimes, two males in the barb family will indulge in what could only be called a "dance," twirling around each other in a seemingly happy fashion.

LEARNING TO DO "TRICKS"

Fish are capable of intelligent behavior and do learn by association. Even the smallest aquarium fishes may learn to come to the side of the tank when their owner taps gently on it, or will swim to the top to beg for food on cue. Some of the larger aquarium fish can be taught to do "tricks," or respond to certain stimuli. Dr. Stoskopf tells of some fish he worked with that learned to swim through hoops on command.

In the August 1989 issue of *Freshwater and Marine Aquarium,* Margaret Hehman-Smith reported on an experiment in which koi were actually trained to hit a lever that rang a bell to signal for food. Dr. Donald Leon Smith, who conducted the experiment, concluded that the behavioral differences between fish, birds, and mammals are negligible when it comes to their ability to learn.

Fish keepers who might want to experiment with training their charges should remember that food is probably the only viable reward to which most fish will respond.

PART TWO

Housing Fish

3

Aquariums

An aquarium is, of course, the first thing that you think of in the way of equipment for tropical fish. Unless you are planning on keeping extremely rare, valuable fish, this and other necessary accessories will represent your largest initial monetary investment. So, before you begin, it's wise to think about just how much money you want to spend on your new hobby. Then you can shop around and make your decisions intelligently.

A Reliable Dealer

Before talking about kinds of aquariums and other equipment, a word to the wise about fish stores. Although you will not be ready to actually choose your fish and stock your aquarium for a while, this is a very good time to find a dealer with whom you can work well throughout all of the steps in your fish-keeping activities. A good dealer can be an invaluable source of information about the purchase of both equipment and fish, and can often help you out of difficulties as you go along.

For reasons that will be explained in more detail in *Chapter Eight: A Source,* the best place to buy fish is a small, personal, "Mom & Pop" establishment. A dealer-owner who takes pride in his livestock, knows something about the fish that he sells, and gets to know his customers will be helpful to you throughout your fish-keeping experience.

Because of their ability to buy in volume, chain discount stores and mail-order houses are usually able to offer you a much better deal on hard goods than a small privately owned store can. But if you buy your supplies from a discount store and have a problem later on, you'll have no redress. As Dr. Paul Loiselle, Assistant Curator of Freshwater Fishes at the New York Aquarium, points out, "It pays to support your local fish dealer. Don't desert him for the sake of a few dollars by buying equipment at a discount house and then expect the dealer to bail you out when something goes wrong." It's best to find a good, reliable private dealer and stick with him for all of your needs.

Aquarium Placement

One of the most important things to decide before you go out to buy an aquarium is, Where are you going to put it? That may seem like pretty elementary advice, but it's something that many people don't give proper consideration.

The size of the tank that you get will be influenced, at least to a certain extent, by where it will be located. One thing that you need to consider is that even acrylic aquariums are very heavy when they are filled. A gallon of water weighs over eight pounds. Add to this the weight of the aquarium itself, the gravel, stand, cover and lights, and other equipment and even a small ten-gallon tank will be 100 or more pounds. A 50-gallon tank can easily weigh more than 500 pounds when filled! Also, if the tank is made of glass, the larger the tank, the thicker (and therefore heavier) the glass must be to withstand the pressure of the water inside. Most ordinary pieces of household furniture aren't strong enough for any but the smallest tank. And, although a stand will help to distribute the weight of a large tank evenly, many floors aren't strong enough to support this kind of concentrated weight. Bear in mind also that the tank will need to be level.

In addition to the weight consideration, you will want to find a place to put your tank where it will have ample space around it—on each side and at the back—for equipment and ease of handling. Remember that once your tank is filled you won't be able to move it no matter how small it is, so you must have access around and behind it. Another reason for plenty of peripheral space is to allow air to circulate freely around the tank to offset the heat generated by the lights and other equipment.

Don't forget that your tank will need something to stand on. If you do want to place it on a piece of sturdy furniture, you should plan to put something underneath the tank to protect the surface of the furniture in case of leaks or spills. A tank that is larger than 20 gallons should usually have its own stand.

Because you'll need to carefully maintain a constant temperature inside the tank, an aquarium should never be placed where it will be in a draft from a door, window, or heating/air-conditioning vent. Direct sunlight is not desirable either. Not only will it heat up the tank excessively, but it will encourage the rampant growth of algae.

Lights, heater, filter, and so forth all run by electricity, so you'll want to be sure that there are outlets near the tank location.

In addition to all of these considerations, the location of

your tank should also be aesthetically pleasing and practical. You certainly want to be able to see it easily, but at the same time you have to think about your furniture and floor coverings. Water will undoubtedly splash during fill-up and necessary changes, and other fish-keeping chores will create wear and tear on nearby furniture and rugs. If you have valuable antiques or rugs in your living room, perhaps you'll want to find another location for your aquarium.

Aquarium Size and Shape

If you are not severely limited as to aquarium size by placement and cost considerations, it's always best to choose a larger, rather than smaller, tank.

The environment inside a small tank is much more fragile than that in a larger one. Any problems that may arise in a fish tank will be more concentrated and will become more serious much more quickly in a small amount of water. A sudden temperature change due to a malfunctioning heater, pollution caused by a broken filter, disease organisms that have been introduced by a new fish, and so forth will create life-threatening conditions much more quickly in a ten-gallon tank than they will in a larger tank in which they will be more diluted and take longer to spread. Thus, a 20-gallon aquarium is easier to maintain than a ten-gallon aquarium, and so on.

However, if you have very limited space and a small budget, many people feel that a ten-gallon tank can be perfectly satisfactory as a "starter" aquarium for small freshwater tropicals, as long as you don't overstock it and are very careful to keep the water in good condition. Novelty miniaquariums that hold only three or four gallons of water are sometimes sold in department stores and through mail order. They are much too small for more than one or two very hardy little fish and are often not heated or filtered properly.

Some people use the amount of water in a tank to gauge the number of fish that it can support. The usual rule of thumb is that one gallon of water should be allowed for each inch of fish (a fish's length is calculated minus its tail). However, water capacity should not be the primary way to measure a tank's ability to maintain fish. The most important consideration for fish health is surface area. Commercial fish breeders/farmers, for instance, often house their fish in large, very shallow (about a foot deep) outdoor vats that have very large surface areas. It's at the water's surface where the exchange of oxygen and carbon dioxide occurs. That is, the dissolved oxygen that the fish need to breathe is replenished in the water while the carbon dioxide that they expel evaporates from it. Without this important exchange, the fish would asphyxiate. Although they do little to remove waste gasses dissolved in the water, airstones (see *Chapter Four*), which create bubbles which break at the water's surface, will facilitate this gas exchange to a certain extent, but the surface area must still be large enough for this to occur. The number of fish that can be accommodated in a tank is determined by the square inches of the tank's surface (calculated by multiplying the tank's width by its length), rather than by the amount of water it can hold, which varies according to the water's depth. The general rule of thumb is that one square foot of water surface is required for each inch of tropical fish. Tall, thin novelty tanks, for example, and bowl-shaped aquariums with sides that slant inward at the top have a very limited fish-supporting capacity no matter how much water they can hold.

If you have already decided on a particular type or types of fish that you will want to house in your aquarium, you will want to bear in mind the particular space needs of the potential occupants when you purchase an aquarium. See *Chapter Eight* for more about this and consult with your dealer.

Kinds of Aquariums

Old-fashioned, metal-framed glass aquariums in which pieces of glass are attached to metal frames with putty are still available. They are sturdy and inexpensive and are certainly fine for beginners with small collections of freshwater fish. They cannot be used for marine aquariums because the saltwater will cause the metal frames to corrode.

All-glass aquariums consisting of plates of glass sealed together with silicone rubber adhesive are now used more often. They afford an unhindered view of the fish, are sturdy and long-lasting, and have no metal parts to corrode. Some are trimmed with plastic edges.

Molded acrylic aquariums appeared on the scene fairly recently. They come in attractive shapes with their own stands and may have baked-in colored backgrounds. Although they are sturdy, they are lighter than glass aquariums of the same size. The only problem is that they are easier to scratch than glass is and some kinds may become cloudy-looking after a while.

There are many different kinds of aquariums available if you look around. You can get an aquarium that is built into a cabinet, for instance, or you can have an aquarium custom-built to suit your own space and decor requirements. Some people even construct their own aquariums. But, whatever kind of aquarium you choose, remember that it will be the eventual home of your fish and needs to meet their requirements above all other considerations.

A Quarantine/Hospital Tank

A quarantine and/or hospital tank is an important investment in the health of any fish collection, although it is almost always overlooked by neophyte fish keepers. This is a tank into which any new fish that you buy should be put before it is added to your collection, in order to be sure that it isn't carrying any disease(s).

The new fish should stay in this tank for two weeks. According to Dr. Loiselle, there's virtually no fish complaint that won't show up in that length of time. Therefore, if no complaint or disease appears after two weeks, you can safely add the new fish to your tank without fear of contaminating the other residents. Some people recommend that you keep the water in a quarantine tank about five-to-ten degrees warmer than you would normally do because the warmer water will cause any disease organisms that are present to develop more quickly.

This tank can also be useful as an "isolation ward"—a hospital facility if one of your fish does develop an illness. In it you can treat the sick individual without worrying about disturbing the other fish, killing your live plants with medications, or allowing whatever infection to spread to your whole collection.

The tank needn't be large: five gallons is adequate for most fish, and auxiliary equipment should be kept to a minimum. Little if any gravel is needed, and no plants or other decorations should be in the tank. All that's necessary is a good heater, a filter, and a cover so that the fish don't jump out. This small tank should be running all the time, biologically balanced and so forth (See *Chapter Eleven*) so that it is always ready to receive a newcomer or patient.

If you always use a quarantine tank when introducing new fish into your aquarium, set up and maintain your main aquarium properly, and select your stock carefully, Dr. Loiselle feels that you should be able to avoid most disease problems. (More about diseases in *Chapter Twelve*.)

4

Aquarium Equipment

In addition to the aquarium itself you will, of course, need to purchase various pieces of equipment in order to keep your fish's environment healthy and comfortable. Some things—a cover, heater, filter and air pump, for instance—are essential to the aquarium inhabitants' well-being. Other pieces of equipment are not absolutely necessary for the fish, but most fish keepers find them desirable. A light, gravel, airstone, and various water test kits fall into this category. Decorations, such as plants, backdrops, and tank furnishings are covered in the next chapter.

Experienced aquarists advise first-time fish keepers to go easy in the beginning. Don't buy every piece of "cute" tank furnishing that you see. Stick to the basics and add other things after you see what you want once you set up your tank and get your fish acclimated.

A word of caution about equipment that will be inside your tank. Be sure that nothing that you put into your aquarium can turn into a death trap for a fish. Curious fish like to explore, and many shy nocturnal fish like to hide.

The narrow space between a hanging water heater and the aquarium glass may seem the perfect hiding place to a catfish, for instance. If a fish becomes jammed behind a heater it can be badly burned or killed, and a fish that has to struggle to extricate itself from any small space will probably not survive for long. Be sure to either allow plenty of room around equipment so that the largest of your fish can get through it easily, or anchor it firmly against the glass with silicone sealant so that there's no space at all.

Covers, Hoods, Lights, and Lighting

Whether or not you plan to use a light for your aquarium, a cover glass is essential. It will keep dust and other objects from getting into the tank and will help to keep the water's surface from cooling off. More important, it will prevent your fish from jumping out!

For ease of feeding, most cover glasses are made in two pieces, or have a small opening cut into them. If you also use a hood with a built-in light for your tank, a cover underneath will prevent it from getting wet due to condensation and splashing. A cover glass is also much easier to keep clean than a hood is.

Hoods with reflectors and light fixtures built in are available to fit all standard-size tanks, and most people opt to light their tanks so that they can see the fish better. Hoods usually fit over the entire top of the tank, are hinged for easy access to the tank, and have openings or vents in them to allow heat from the lights to escape. Fluorescent bulbs are recommended for fish tanks. They are less expensive to operate than incandescent bulbs are, but the most important reason to use fluorescent rather than incandescent bulbs is because the latter burn very hot. Not only will incandescent bulbs heat up the aquarium water excessively, but they will make the hood too hot to touch and can become a fire hazard if left on for hours at a time. All but the smallest hood-lights have space for two or more fluorescent tubes, so that different-colored bulbs can be mixed for the best effect. Even though you may not notice it at first, fluorescent bulbs lose power after a period of continuous use, so it's a good idea to change your bulbs at least once a year for optimum efficiency and light production.

The placement of artificial lighting is an important consideration. Hoods with built-in lights are usually designed with the lights themselves located toward the back of the aquarium so that shadows don't interfere with fish visibility. Some people add special lighting effects with spotlights or decorative underwater accent lighting that consists of acrylic forms placed in the water and lighted from behind and outside the tank.

AMOUNT OF LIGHT

You will have to experiment in order to find just the right amount of light for your tank. Because water absorbs light and cuts its strength you will need more light than you might expect so that some reaches the bottom of the tank. However, if a light is too intense and is left on for too long, it will encourage algae to grow too fast.

On the other hand, if you want to grow real plants in your aquarium, you'll have to provide them with sufficient light to stay healthy and to encourage photosynthesis (the process in which plants absorb carbon dioxide and release oxygen).

Although there are usually twelve to fourteen hours of sunlight each day in the tropics, remember that thick vegetation and murky water filter and modify the actual amount of light that reaches most tropical plants and fish. Thus, while some aquarists recommend up to fourteen hours of artificial light a day for an aquarium, others feel that a lot less is plenty. If you have nonnatural plantings and simply want to view your fish, eight to ten hours of daily artificial lighting should be fine. In all but the darkest corners, your fish will get sufficient natural light during the course of the day to meet their needs. Commercial fish farmers/breeders rarely use any artificial lighting at all for their fish, but rely on natural light alone. In warm climates they keep their fish outdoors; in cooler areas they house them in large sheds that have glass roofs. Some fish are very skittish when lights are very bright. Brian Morris, an expert on discus fish from Clearwater, Florida, recommends diffusing the light for discus by placing some kind of filtering material between the light and the cover of the tank.

Most people use an automatic timer for their fish tank lights so that they will go on and off at the same time every day. It really doesn't matter to the fish when the light goes on, so you can time your lighting to suit your own schedule, as long as you're consistent. In order to avoid startling very skittish, shy fish you should also time a room lamp to go on shortly before the overhead tank light does (and off after it does) so that the fish can get used to the light change gradually, just as they would in a natural habitat. Many people also recommend using overhead lighting very sparingly for a while in order to reduce stress when fish are moved to a new tank or after new fish are introduced to an aquarium.

Heaters and Thermometers

In almost every climate, it's critical to have a reliable heater that will keep your tropical aquarium at the proper temperature all of the time without undue fluctuations. Because fish are "cold-blooded," they cannot regulate their own body temperatures and are dependent on the temperature of the water around them to maintain proper body heat. In a natural setting, water temperature changes occur gradually because of the volume of the water. But in an aquarium environment, water will cool or heat quite quickly. How fast it does depends on the size of the tank. Sudden temperature fluctuations are extremely stressful to fish and make them very susceptible to disease. Some fish are more delicate than others when it comes to precise temperature ranges, but all tropical fish need to have their water maintained at a comfortable level, around 75°F or more. Even if you live in a warm climate, you should have a heater for your tank in case of sudden drops in temperature. If you live in a very warm climate you will have to be sure that your tank doesn't become overheated, especially in the summer, by keeping it in an air-conditioned room and shading it from the sun.

Nowadays, combined heater-thermostats have replaced the separate units previously used in aquariums. Once you set them, they will turn on and off automatically in order to maintain the water at the desired temperature. Two kinds are most often available. Those that hang on the side of the tank, and those that can be completely submerged in the water, where they are usually attached to the side or back of the aquarium with suction cups. Sufficient wattage is necessary to heat the amount of water that you have in your tank. Many people with large tanks choose to use two heaters, one at each end of the aquarium, in order to ensure even heat. Estimates of the necessary wattage per gallon vary widely, from four to ten watts per gallon of water in a tank, so it's best to rely on your dealer for advice. The number of watts you will need depends, in part, on how warm you want the water to be and the temperature in the surrounding room.

MAINTAINING HEAT

Many people place their aquariums in the warmest room in the house in order to reduce electrical use, especially in very cold climates. If the furnace in your house goes down at night or if you live in a climate where it gets very cold in the winter, you can help to offset some heat loss from your aquarium by using some kind of insulating material (sheets of polystyrene, for example) underneath your tank and in back of it. Newspapers also make very good insulating material and can be wrapped around an aquarium in the event of a sudden power failure or severe temperature drop.

In an emergency power outage, water temperature loss may be gradual at first, but should be monitored carefully. If it starts to drop, the best way to keep it warm is to place sealed glass containers of hot water in the aquarium. Be careful to avoid overflow by removing some water ahead of time. Never pour hot water directly into the tank—the sudden temperature change will probably kill the fish.

KINDS OF HEATERS

Up until recently, the only kind of aquarium heaters available were those with bimetal temperature sensors. These metal contacts, or breaker points, move apart and together at the slightest variation of degree and cause the heating unit to turn on and off constantly in order to maintain the proper water temperature. Eventually, these metal contacts wear and may stick, especially if the room temperature rises suddenly, causing the heater to run continuously. If this is not corrected, the fish are literally boiled! This is a common enough occurrence so that it is referred to frequently in publications dealing with fish keeping. Fortunately, there are now solid-state heaters with electronic sensors that are immersed in the water and have no moving parts to wear out. They are very accurate and easy to set and, although they are about twice as expensive as other heaters, are considered by most experienced fish keepers to be well worth the price.

THERMOMETERS

In order to know if your heater is functioning correctly, you will need a thermometer in place so that you can constantly monitor the water's temperature. There are several kinds of aquarium thermometers on the market. The least expensive and easiest to read is a self-sticking liquid crystal strip thermometer that adheres to the glass outside of the aquarium. Round dial-type thermometers can also stick onto the outside of the tank. Floating glass thermometers made for aquariums are inexpensive and simple to use. To compensate for possible variations in either the thermometer or heater, you should calibrate them at a known temperature before you add your fish. If the thermometer consistently reads one or two degrees high, for instance, you will be able to set the heater accordingly.

Serious breeders, and people who keep valuable fish that have very specific water temperature requirements, like Brian Morris with his discus fish, prefer to use highly accurate thermometers that are designed primarily for laboratory or photographic use. These sealed glass tubes can be immersed in water and placed at the bottom of the tank for easy viewing. They are available in photographic supply stores or mail-order catalogs.

Pumps and Filters

Although they are usually two separate pieces of equipment, pumps and filters are listed together because they work together. As a matter of fact, they are often lumped together under the single heading "Filters" in many books and articles. Without a pump, water would not flow through the filter. Appropriate tubing to connect the filter and pump and a valve or valves to prevent the water from going backward into the pump are also part of the equipment that you'll need when setting up a filtering system.

Briefly, this is how they work together. In *Chapter Three: Aquariums,* we talked about the fact that it is at the surface of the water that the gas exchange occurs (oxygen in, carbon dioxide out). The water in a fish tank must move in order to facilitate this exchange at the surface. In other words, it must be continuously circulated and aerated. That's one function of the pump. But, at the same time, wastes and impurities produced by the fish must be removed from the water through a filter that often contains a straining-type medium. The pump is necessary to force the water through the filter and back out into the tank. At the same time that the filter removes harmful elements from the water, it is also a storage area for bacteria that are necessary and beneficial for the fish. (More about these necessary bacteria in *Chapter Six: Water*) The pump is generally left on all of the time for maximum efficiency and water maintenance and, if it is outside the tank, must have sufficient space around it to allow air to circulate freely.

KINDS OF PUMPS

There are two basic types of air-driven pumps for aquariums. Vibrator pumps that have oscillating diaphragms to move the air are quite simple and require little maintenance, but inexpensive models may be quite noisy. Piston pumps are quieter in general, more expensive, and do require some maintenance. However, if you plan to run more than one filter or other equipment off your pump, a piston pump is preferable.

The size and type of pump that you will need depends on the size of your aquarium and the kind of fish that you plan to keep in it. Fish that produce a lot of waste, such as cichlids, require heavier duty filtering than cleaner fish, for example. A too-weak pump clearly won't do the job, but a pump that's too strong may create too much water motion for many fish and will continuously disturb the aquarium water.

Some pumps are designed for use outside the aquarium; others are submersible and are placed inside the tank. Generally speaking, submersible pumps are less costly to buy, but may be more expensive to run. New products are always appearing on the market, however, and the kind of pump that you select should be based on your own preference and particular setup. Your dealer is the best person to advise you about which pump type and capacity will fit your needs.

CANISTER, OR INTERNAL POWER FILTERS

There are combination pump-filters that use various filtering mediums. They are either open boxes or canisters and can be mounted inside or outside of the tank. Dirty water is drawn directly into the filter through the filtering medium and the cleaned water is pumped back out into the aquarium. They are usually very powerful, have a large water flow capacity, and are recommended for large tanks.

KINDS OF FILTERS

The various kinds of filters on the market come in so many different sizes and shapes that it can be very confusing. Actually, the sizes and shapes are not as important as knowing about the three major *ways* in which filters work.

Mechanical filtration is the simplest. It merely removes floating debris from the water by means of a filtering agent such as floss or foam of some kind, which must be removed and cleaned under running water frequently—usually once a week—and replaced when it becomes oversoiled. Mechanical filtration is often combined with chemical filtration, which removes dissolved solids from the water by filtering it through activated carbon. The carbon absorbs things such as fish wastes and other chemicals from the water. Carbon soon becomes saturated and is no longer viable, so it is necessary to replace it every few weeks. It can be hard to tell when the carbon is no longer doing its job. Although some people say that heating the carbon in an oven will reactivate it, most experts recommend replacing it altogether. To avoid unnecessary changes, you can get a test kit to measure the carbon's efficiency.

If you want to alter the chemical composition of the water in your aquarium you can use your mechanical or chemical filter to do so. For instance, you can add peat to the filter to make the water more acid.

Biological filtration works on a completely different principle. Instead of drawing the water out of the tank and through a filtering medium that removes harmful wastes and chemicals, it works within the tank itself to promote the buildup of beneficial bacteria in the gravel, on a sponge, or other material. The bacteria neutralizes harmful wastes and chemicals by breaking them down into harmless compounds. Bacterial filters should only be cleaned if they become too clogged to operate efficiently, because cleaning will destroy the beneficial bacteria.

The most frequently used biological filtration system is an undergravel filter. An undergravel filter consists of a flat porous or slotted plate that is placed on the bottom of the aquarium underneath an inch or two of gravel, through which the water is forced from above by a pump. Alternately, the power pump forces the air through the filter from below, preventing it from becoming clogged by debris from the tank. This is called reverse-flow undergravel filtration and is favored by many people. In each case, the water can also be mechanically and/or chemically filtered outside of the tank in order to remove excess detritus. If reverse-flow filtration is used alone, there will not be sufficient air bubbles rising to the surface and it will be necessary to use one or more airstones.

Instead of undergravel filters, Dr. Loiselle highly recommends sponge-type bacterial filters that utilize internal power filters. They hang on the inside of the aquarium and use removable sponge pads as filter mediums. He finds them preferable to undergravel filters for several reasons. First, if you have fish that like to dig, they will disturb the gravel on the bottom of the tank, and anything that removes gravel from the top of the filter plate will immediately reduce the efficiency of an undergravel filter. Second, once an undergravel filter is in place, it is immobile. If you need to treat the tank with some kind of medication that kills bacteria, or if the filter becomes completely clogged with debris and must be cleaned, the entire tank will have to be dismantled and you'll be back to square one as far as biological filtration goes—you'll have killed all of the bacteria.

With sponge-type filters, you have more surface area for bacteria to grow on than you do with a filter plate that covers the entire bottom of most tanks. An additional advantage is that you can remove one sponge that has been inoculated with bacteria from your established tank, attach it to a new filter in a quarantine tank, for instance, and immediately establish a biologically balanced tank.

Sponge-like filters may not be as readily available as other types of filters are. For some reason, most dealers don't recommend them. But if you think that you would like to try one, ask.

Airstones

In general, separate airstones are not necessary in a fish tank. Most filters are designed to provide sufficient aeration (a stream of bubbles that break at the surface and facilitate gas exchange). But, in the event of a power filter breakdown, if you have no other supplementary source of aeration, your fish will soon die. So, many people do use an airstone that works off of a separate pump as an "insurance policy."

Some people also like the look of the large bubbles that most airstones produce. Airstones are made in a wide variety of novelty shapes to suit all tastes, from belching hippos and clams to bubbling deep-sea divers.

Water Test Kits

We will talk more about the chemistry of your aquarium water in *Chapter Six,* but while discussing necessary equipment water test kits must be included. Since there is no way that you can judge water chemistry in your aquarium by just looking at it, you will need to invest in one or more inexpensive water test kits.

Test kits are available to measure: the pH (acidity or alkalinity) of the water; the mineral content or hardness of the water, represented by TDS (Total Dissolved Solvents), or DH, which is the German hardness scale and is most often used; and nitrate concentration (usually caused by excessive ammonia). According to Dr. Loiselle, this is the single most important test of water quality in a freshwater tropical aquarium. There are several other kinds of test kits that measure different water components, but you only need them under special circumstances. Don't allow yourself to be talked into buying them if you have no particular use for them.

Test kits come with complete instructions and are generally used to test the water quality when the aquarium is first set up, before the fish are added, and each time that the water is changed, so that the water quality can be adjusted if necessary. It's a good idea to test the water at the same time of day because the water chemistry is affected by the temperature of the water, amount of light, and other factors that will change.

Gravel

According to some people, gravel should be included in the "purely decorative furnishings" category and is not needed in a fish tank at all. Those with fish that produce a heavy amount of waste, such as many cichlids, often prefer to keep the bottom of the aquarium free of gravel for ease of cleaning. Others feel that gravel makes up part of the natural environment of fish and, of course, it is essential if you want to use an undergravel filter.

You will also need gravel to anchor live plants if you want to include them in your aquarium. Some bottom-dwelling fish want gravel to bury themselves in and other fish bury their eggs in it.

Gravel should be smooth-edged so as not to injure fish, and not too coarse or it will trap uneaten particles of food too readily. Nor should it be too fine or it may get into the filtering system and block it.

Many aquarists choose natural, plain sandy-colored gravel in the fish tank. Dark-colored gravel is preferred by many fish that are used to muddy or rocky bottoms and it makes all fish feel secure because it provides them with a natural camouflage. (The dark line on top of fish's backs matches the bottom and makes them hard to see from above.) If you prefer, you can now purchase gravel in a variety of bright colors that are intended to provide flattering backgrounds for different kinds of freshwater fish.

It is important to purchase gravel intended specifically for aquarium use. Other kinds of sands and gravels may contain minerals and other materials that could alter the water chemistry and might even be poisonous to your fish. All gravel should be rinsed thoroughly in a sieve or bucket until the water runs completely clear before it is put into the aquarium.

Gravel is usually placed in the bottom of the aquarium in a sloping fashion, deepest at the back. If you're using an undergravel filter, you'll need two or more inches of gravel throughout the bottom of the tank.

Other Equipment

There are a few other pieces of equipment that may be needed in an emergency and are often forgotten by first-time fish keepers.

Dr. Staskopf remarked, "It's amazing. People spend hundreds of dollars on an aquarium and fish and fancy foods, and they don't own a $1.59 net." Although there are substitutes that can be used to catch a live fish or remove a dead one from the tank, a net is certainly the easiest and quickest tool to use—two nets, used in opposition, can be even better. A net will also come in handy if anything that doesn't belong in the tank falls in, and the handle can be a useful tool to reach an uprooted plant or other decoration. Be sure that the net you purchase has a long enough handle to reach the bottom of the tank easily, without getting your sleeve wet, and is large enough to hold your biggest fish.

Another essential accessory is at least one bucket, or large dishpan, in which to carry water for changes, to siphon water into, or to put a fish or plant in temporarily. The housekeeping or dishwashing bucket or pan that you already have can't be used, because plastic readily absorbs chemicals from cleaning agents. You need to have at least one large receptacle that is reserved for fish-keeping use alone.

Buy at least a double length of plastic tubing and several extra clamps, in case yours break or spring a leak. Couplings where hoses attach to pumps, filters, and so forth tend to split after a while and it's always a good idea to have extra on hand.

In the non-emergency department, but good to have on hand, are cleaning/housekeeping tools, such as a glass scraper to get rid of excess algae, and a long siphon or basting tube to remove debris from the bottom of the tank. A specially designed gravel cleaner may come in handy, too. A magnifying glass for close-up observations is extremely useful, as are measuring spoons and cups and a notebook reserved for your fish-keeping observations.

You may see all kinds of other fish-keeping equipment for sale, from gloves to wear when taking care of your aquarium to handy instruments for trimming plants under-water. Most are not needed or desirable. You will startle and upset your fish less if you use your bare hands when you have to work in the tank, rather than wearing brightly col-ored gloves. When your fingers aren't enough, a simple tweezer or pair of blunt scissors will usually work better to trim plants than a fancy long-handled tool. Use your judg-ment and purchase only the equipment that you really need.

5

Plants and Other Aquarium Furnishings

Although there are some people who prefer a "bare bones" approach to fish tanks, most individuals who keep fish do so for pleasure and want to create a naturalistic, attractive-looking aquarium. Although fish tank decorations are not essential for the health of the fish, aquarium furnishings do provide them with protection, privacy, and a sense of security. At the same time, tank furnishings can help to hide or disguise many pieces of in-tank equipment.

Backdrops

Backdrops are used for purely aesthetic reasons. They hide the "works" that are usually housed behind the aquarium, and provide a background against which the fish in the aquarium can be better seen. They differ widely.

Many of the new acrylic aquariums are made with an opaque, baked-in, colored back panel, which makes any other backdrop unnecessary.

Some people opt to paint a background directly onto the

outside of the back aquarium glass—either a solid color, design, or underwater scene. Others build dioramas of rocks and/or a combination of natural materials that they attach to the outside of the back panel with silicone adhesive.

For the noncreative, there are colorful, ready-made scenes and designs printed on stiff paper that are prepared to be attached to the back of the aquarium. The advantage of this kind of backdrop is that it's inexpensive and can be easily changed when you tire of it.

Whatever backdrop you choose, remember not to make it too busy or obtrusive—you want to be able to see the fish in front of it. If you plan to use abundant planting and/or other tank furnishings, the backdrop design will probably be mostly hidden anyway.

Live Plants

Live plants used to be considered essential to the maintenance of a healthy environment in a fish tank because they aid in the gas exchange and help to keep the aquarium free of waste material. With modern filtration and aeration systems, plants are no longer needed for these reasons.

Plants do provide excellent hiding places and spawning sites for many fish, and will help prevent fish from jumping out of the tank. They encourage the growth of algae and other microorganisms that are excellent for fry. What's more, they can be a very attractive addition to the aquarium if they are healthy and well kept.

Plants do not do well with some kinds of fish. Many large cichlids, for example, will uproot and devour very quickly any natural plants in the tank. So, although they do make good eating for these fish, it is far more economical to give the fish some lettuce to eat instead and to furnish the tank with something else that doesn't taste as good (see *page 60*).

There are literally hundreds of different kinds of plants that are sold for aquarium use, and new specimens are introduced regularly. They come in a wide variety of colors, shapes, and sizes and because they naturally grow in many different environments (rivers, lakes, swamps), often have very specific requirements as to the warmth, cleanliness, and chemistry of the water, and amount of light.

Most plants do best in a tank that's understocked with fish. For example, Amazon sword plants are very popular and are often recommended by dealers. But they require very soft water and won't do well in a crowded tank when the water contains a lot of wastes. Some plants, on the other hand, such as the banana plant, Java fern, water sprite, and broad-leafed Indian fern, are quite hardy and forgiving and can tolerate most kinds of water, as will some of the popular floating plants such as water lettuce, floating fern, and the tough-leaved hornwart which can also withstand some pretty tough nibbling assaults. If you plan to use live plants in your aquarium, you can save yourself a lot of trouble and expense if you find out about the different kinds and their requirements before buying.

KINDS OF LIVE AQUARIUM PLANTS

Aquarium plants come in several forms. Among them are plants with roots that will be buried in the gravel, rooted plants that are placed in the aquarium in pots, cuttings, or plants that do not have roots but are bunched together and are usually held at the bottom by lead strips that give them weight so that they will stay in place in the gravel, and floating plants.

Most floating aquarium plants have small, hairy, trailing

roots that make excellent hiding places for fry and small surface-swimmers. They can help to keep "jumpers" in the water and provide shade to the inhabitants below. They grow very fast and, unless you have one or more avid plant-eaters in your fish collection, you must trim them severely and regularly or they will overwhelm the aquarium. They need to be protected from too much heat from the overhead lights by a cover. Some won't tolerate too much dampness from condensation that will form on the bottom of the glass, however, so the cover needs to be vented to allow moisture to escape.

Rooted aquarium plants usually have very small root systems. Most do not get nourishment through their roots like nonwater plants, but feed through their leaves. Some are planted directly in the bottom gravel, but others will attach themselves to rocks, logs, and even to other plants. They can be helped to root on these mediums if you tie them gently in place with a piece of nylon thread or fishing line.

Potted plants are sometimes favored by people who have very strong undergravel filters or fish that are determined diggers. When they are buried in the gravel, the pots are not visible and the plants are harder to uproot. Potted plants are also easy to move around in the aquarium if you change your mind about your planting arrangement. (It's bad for plants to be uprooted and moved too often.) Pots are useful if you want to encourage your plants to grow quickly with plant plugs or other rooting material.

BUYING LIVE AQUARIUM PLANTS AND PREPARING THEM FOR PLANTING

Unless you select really large specimen plants for your tank, most live aquarium plants are not very expensive. But don't let their fairly low cost tempt you into buying too many. In the first place, many plants will grow very fast and soon take up all of your fish's swimming space. Second, if the plants don't do well you won't have made too big an investment and can start over with another variety that may be better suited to your particular aquarium. Get a few attractive plants at first and see how they do—you can always add more later.

Select your plants with some care from a reliable dealer. Keep them damp in a plastic bag or a covered bowl of water until you're ready to plant them. Before you put new plants in your aquarium, rinse them thoroughly and inspect each root and leaf carefully for snails and snail eggs. Some people advocate dipping plants in a mild, nontoxic sterilizing agent such as alum before you introduce them into an aquarium, but this doesn't seem necessary if you've purchased them from a reliable source and they look healthy. Remove any wilted leaves and dried-up roots with a sharp plant-clipper and trim the roots neatly.

KEEPING AQUARIUM PLANTS HEALTHY

Undoubtedly, the well-being of the fish in your aquarium is your primary concern, so you can't alter the temperature, chemical balance, or temperature of the water to suit your plants.

You can keep your plants neat and trim if you remove any dead leaves or stems by hand each week and cut or break off any too-long pieces. If your plants in pots are not doing well, you can move them around so that they get a different amount of light or less water motion, for instance.

There are fertilizers and plant foods on the market that are specially made for aquatic plants, but be very careful because although these fertilizing agents may not be toxic for fish, they will alter the chemical balance of the water. Most aquatic plants obtain sufficient nutrients from the water that they live in.

If aquatic plants turn very pale, they are probably not getting enough light each day. Without sufficient light aquatic plants will also absorb too much oxygen from the water. When there is light, plants go through a process that we mentioned in *Chapter Four* called photosynthesis, in which they absorb carbon dioxide and release oxygen. When it is dark the process is reversed, and could be very harmful to your fish if it occurs for too long each day.

Plastic Plants

Except for an occasional rinsing off, artificial plastic plants require little if any care, and are the choice of people who like the look and advantages of a planted aquarium but don't want to have to deal with live plants or can't keep them for one reason or another. They are resistant to the nibbling of fish, have no water or temperature preferences, keep their color and looks for a long time, and are not expensive.

They also serve many of the same purposes for which people often buy live plants. They provide hiding places, and fish will spawn on them. Algae will grow on their leaves, and they give shade. The only role that they don't share with live plants is that of food.

All plastic plants used to be obviously fake and not very attractive, but better manufacturing methods have now been able to produce some artificial plants for aquariums that look amazingly real when they're in place in the water. They come in a wide variety of shapes, sizes, and colors and are usually made with a clear plastic base plate that can be easily anchored in the gravel.

There are still some pretty bad-looking artificial aquarium

plants on the market, but try to reserve judgment until you see some good ones in an aquarium—you may be surprised!

Rocks and Driftwood

Rocks and pieces of driftwood can be used in an aquarium along with plants or by themselves to create an attractive setting for your fish and provide them with plenty of nooks and crannies to explore, rest, and spawn in. Some fish, such as African lake cichlids for instance, come from areas where they have lots of natural rocky caves and tree roots in which to hide and will especially appreciate a tank that provides them with the same environment.

ROCKS

No matter how many pretty rocks you may have collected in your travels, it's best not to use them in your aquarium unless you're really sure where they come from and what they're made of.

Rocks with any metal ore in them are to be avoided, as are limestone rocks and calcareous (chalky) rocks that will make the aquarium water harder. Hard, nonsoluble rocks such as quartz, sandstone, shale, and slate are best, but they should be boiled and scrubbed to remove any residues that might be on the surface and filed to remove any sharp edges.

To be on the safe side, you can usually purchase attractive rocks that are sold specifically for aquarium use at your fish dealer's.

Be careful when you place rocks in your aquarium. Any large rocks, or rocks that you wish to stand at an angle, should be carefully glued to the bottom or side of the tank with silicone so that they can't possibly fall over. Be sure that any space behind the rock is either small enough so that none of your fish can get into it, or large enough so that they can't become stuck.

DRIFTWOOD

Aged tree roots and driftwood are very attractive, natural additions to any aquarium. Again, it's usually safer to purchase wood of any kind in a fish supply store rather than using some that you have collected yourself. Wood is very porous, absorbent material and, unless you are absolutely sure about the chemistry of the water it has been in, it's too risky to take a chance on polluting your aquarium with unknown toxins.

Commercially available pieces of wood have usually been thoroughly sanded to remove the outside surface. If you want to be doubly sure that the wood you buy is safe, soak it overnight in a Clorox solution and rinse it thoroughly several times before putting it into your aquarium. You can also coat wood with a nontoxic, waterproof sealing agent.

If the wood you are going to use is not waterlogged it will probably float and must be anchored to the bottom of the tank with glue, or mounted on a heavy, stable base of some sort. The same safety precautions that you use for rocks should be employed when placing large pieces of wood in your aquarium. Be sure that they are well anchored and will withstand prodding and poking by fish and the movement of the water around them.

Other Furnishings

Cork bark is more flexible than wood and can be quite easily bent or shaped to hide tank equipment. It is often available in fish supply stores. Again, to be on the safe side you may want to boil it before adding it to your aquarium.

Plain, baked flowerpots and tiles—either whole ones or pieces—are excellent pieces of aquarium furniture, especially for fish such as discus to lay their eggs on. Flowerpots that have been used for plants may have absorbed some chemicals or fertilizers from the soil, so use only new pots and be sure to rinse them thoroughly before placing them in your aquarium.

Artificial wood, rocks, and so forth that are sold for aquarium use may not look very real outside of the tank. But once they're in place in the water and become covered by algae or plantings, you will be surprised at how real they do look.

Unless you deliberately want to make the aquarium water harder, never use shells, wood, or rocks that you've collected at the beach in a freshwater aquarium. They are full of soluble alkaline salts that no amount of washing can prevent from leaching out into the water.

6

Water

Even in nature, no water is truly pure. Rainwater is the purest, but it picks up particles of pollution as it falls. The chemical makeup of fresh water around the world in lakes, ponds, streams, and rivers differs according to a number of factors. Minerals and gasses are picked up along the way as water flows toward the ocean, decaying vegetation and other wastes are dissolved in the water, and the banks and bottoms also contribute their part in making up the final chemistry of a particular body of water. The amount of motion in the water also affects its makeup, especially the amount of oxygen that it contains—fast-flowing streams and rivers contain a lot of oxygen, while lakes or ponds where there is little or no movement and the water is seldom if ever renewed by rivers or streams have water with very little dissolved oxygen in it. (Remember that the gas exchange occurs at the water's surface.)

The tropical freshwater fish that we keep in aquariums come from various geographical areas and naturally inhabit different kinds of water. Some fish are very particular about the water that they live in, while others are able to do well in almost any kind of water. The water that comes out of our faucets also differs considerably, depending on what part of the world we live in. In order to understand in what ways water can differ and how we can change it if necessary to suit the fish in our care, it's necessary to know something about the various components and qualities of water. Don't ever change water conditions too suddenly or put a fish in a tank with different water conditions than it's used to or you may shock it enough to kill it. Before you become overly worried, though, remember that most of the tropical freshwater fish that are sold in stores nowadays are bred on commercial fish farms in water that usually does not exactly replicate conditions in the wild. What's more, if your fish dealer is located near you, the fish that you buy from him will have been living in water that comes from the same source as yours does.

Before you go out and buy test kits to measure the chemistry of your water, ask your local water supply department about the water in your area. They have tested the water extensively, know exactly what they treat it with to make it safe to drink, and are usually only too happy to supply you with information that will save you a lot of money, time, and worry. Be sure to tell them why you want to know, and ask if they ever bring in water from other areas, or treat the water differently in times of peak demand or during a dry spell, for instance. Don't forget that your copper or lead pipes may contribute some metal traces to your water. Let it run for a few minutes to be sure to flush them out before adding water to your aquarium.

Oxygen and Carbon Dioxide

Animals that live out of the water breathe in air, extract the oxygen from it, and exhale carbon dioxide. Almost all fish have to obtain the oxygen that they need from the water that they live in, and they also exhale carbon dioxide into the water—we have already discussed how they do this in *Chapter One*.

Water contains a lot less oxygen than air does, and the warmer (and saltier) the water, the less oxygen it can hold. Tropical fish have adapted to this to a certain extent, but if the already low oxygen levels in the warm aquarium water drop at all, the fish will be in difficulty and can be observed gasping for air at the surface or staying perfectly still in the water and breathing rapidly with fully opened gill covers. Some fish will even jump out of the tank in an effort to get more oxygen. (Fish can be in distress for other reasons, too—more about this later on.)

Oxygen naturally enters aquarium water two ways. It is manufactured by green plants in the process called photosynthesis, but plants also use up oxygen from the water when it's dark, so they cannot be counted on to supply enough oxygen for the fish. As a matter of fact, if an aquarium is overplanted and underlit the plants may do more harm than good in this respect.

As we've talked about in previous chapters, it's at the surface of the water that the primary exchange of gasses occurs—oxygen enters the water, while carbon dioxide escapes from it. There must be enough water circulation in the tank to provide for sufficient gas exchange at the surface. This is accomplished if the filter-pumping system is adequate for the size of the aquarium and the number and type of its inhabitants. If the tank is severely overcrowded, no amount of aeration will be enough.

If you change your tank setup in any way—buy new equipment or fish, for instance—you should test the water for oxygen and carbon dioxide levels. There are easy-to-use kits on the market for this purpose. If the oxygen is too low, increased aeration will eventually bring the level up. In an emergency situation when you can't wait for this to happen, there are oxygen-enhancing products (made up mostly of hydrogen peroxide) on the market, but be sure to check with your dealer for advice: a sudden change in the oxygen level can be very stressful for fish, and some fish can be badly harmed if the oxygen level becomes too high.

Hard and Soft Water

Water is deemed to be hard or soft according to the amount of mineral salts that it contains. The majority of tropical freshwater fish are used to living in soft water that contains little or no minerals.

Distilled water is the softest water of all because it contains no minerals. If you put fish in pure distilled water, however, they would swell up and burst because of osmosis (see *Chapter One*). Water hardness is measured in two ways—temporary hardness and permanent hardness. The sum of both temporary and permanent hardness in water is what is measured by most test kits. If you boil water, you will remove the temporary hardness by breaking down the dissolved calcium and magnesium bicarbonate, but the permanent hardness (noncarbonate minerals) will remain and must be removed by other means.

There are several different scales used to measure the total hardness or softness of water. One measures TDS—Total Dissolved Solids—in the water. The more commonly used scale is dH—the German hardness scale. It doesn't matter which scale you use as long as you follow the manufacturer's instructions.

The softness or hardness of water can be modified to suit your fish's needs if necessary, but bear in mind that it can be a tricky process and can affect the water in other ways, by changing the pH, for example. So it's best to have expert advice before setting out to change the hardness or softness of the water.

Most water that comes out of the tap in the United States is slightly hard. In addition to boiling it to remove temporary hardness, too-hard water can be softened by diluting it with distilled water or filtering it through peat—both of which will reduce the total hardness of the water. Ion exchange resins used in your filter or a reverse osmosis unit that removes the minerals from the water will alter the permanent hardness of the water.

If you should need to make soft water harder you can add chalk, limestone, or special mineral blocks that are sold in fish supply stores.

Acid and Alkaline Water

Perhaps the most confusing aspect of water for most newcomers to keeping fish is the pH value of the water. A scale on which the acidity or alkalinity of water is measured is pH. Acid water contains more acids than alkalis while alkaline water has more alkalis in it. The pH measurement of water varies inversely depending on the number of hydrogen ions in solution in it. The most acid water will measure 0 on the pH scale; the most alkaline will measure 14. Neutral water, such as distilled water, has a pH of 7. The scale progresses geometrically, thus water with a pH of 8 is ten times more alkaline than distilled water, while a pH of 6 indicates that it is ten times more acidic. It may be easier to remember if you know that lemon juice has a pH of 2, while ammonia has a pH of 12.

Most freshwater tropical fish prefer water with a pH value

between 6.5 (slightly acid) and 7.5 (slightly alkaline). The pH value of water in an aquarium is closely related to the hardness or softness of the water; hard water is usually alkaline and soft water is acidic. If you change the hardness of water you will probably alter the pH value and vice versa. Overcrowding, excessive wastes, and plant decay will make the water more acid, as will the excessive use of peat to soften water. If the pH in your aquarium is too low, you can raise it if you feed less, increase the filtration, change the water more often, and take a few fish out. There are water treatments on the market to alter the pH value of aquarium water—sodium biphosphate will lower it, while sodium bicarbonate will make it higher.

The pH values in a normal aquarium usually vary a bit during the course of a day, so it's best to test the water at the same time of day in order to get a true comparative reading.

Chlorine and Chloramine

Chlorine and ammonia are not found naturally in water, but are added to water to make it safe for drinking. Before treating your aquarium water it is very important to find out what kind of disinfecting agent your water company uses.

In most parts of the United States where free chlorine is used in the water, chlorine is not in the water in excess and doesn't present a serious problem for tropical fish if the water is allowed to sit in an open container for twenty-four or more hours to disperse the chlorine before adding fish. Sun will hasten the dispersion, as will strong aeration. You can tell if there is a good deal of chlorine in the water if you can smell it when it comes out of the tap. In that case, you'll need to use a dechlorinating agent based on sodium thio-sorbate that will bond chemically with the chlorine and neutralize it. If you're in doubt, you can test the water with a chlorine test kit.

In many parts of the country, another substance, called chloramine, a chlorine-ammonia compound, is now being used to treat water. It's used in areas where the water is soft and is drawn from a reservoir in which natural organic material is present because plain chlorine acts with organic materials to form a carcinogenic compound.

Dr. Loiselle says that there are two problems when chloramine is being used. First, you can't smell it and therefore have no way of knowing if it's in the water at all or if it is, how heavy a concentration there is of it. Second, it is much, much more dangerous to fish than free chlorine is. It is much more persistent—that is, it stays in the water longer to do damage. Also, if you treat the water with a standard chlorine-removing agent you will break the bond between the chlorine and the ammonia and will still have a toxic concentration of ammonia in the water.

There are commercial preparations designed to rid the water of chloramine that break the chlorine-ammonia bond, neutralize the chlorine, and form a complex from the ammonia that a biological filter can break down at leisure. But you must know ahead of time what the water department uses to disinfect the water in your area—free chlorine or chloramine.

Other Things That Affect Water Quality

No matter how carefully you adjust the water quality in your aquarium at first, problems can arise to upset the balance. Overcrowding and excessive waste, among other factors, can cause the water to become unhealthy for your fish. These things will be discussed in *Chapter Nine: The Nitrogen Cycle,* and *Chapter Eleven*.

Choosing Fish to Suit Your Water

Changing the basic hardness and pH of the water that comes from the faucet in your area is a time- and money-consuming effort, often fraught with frustration and failure. Water naturally will revert back to its original state unless it is constantly treated.

Dr. Loiselle says, "Unless you are a person whose buttons are pushed by playing in forensic water chemistry, it really isn't worth it. Adjust your fish collection to suit the water in your area." In his opinion, most people spend altogether too much time, effort, and money trying to modify their tap water. In most parts of the country, what comes out of the tap will support a nice selection of freshwater fish without any modification at all, but the selection will be different depending on where you live. If you live on Long Island, where the water has almost no dissolved solids and comes out of the tap with a pH of 5.0, the easiest fish for you to keep would be those that like soft water. Tetras, rasboras, South American dwarf cichlids, angelfish, and discus will all think that the Long Island water is great. If, on the other hand, you live in Austin, Texas, where the water has a pH of 11 and can be aerated down to about 8 at the lowest, then the fish that will do best for you are brackish-water fish such as livebearers and hardwater fish such as African lake cichlids.

If you take Dr. Loiselle's advice, you'll find out about the pH and hardness of the water in your area and choose the fish for your aquarium accordingly, or resign yourself to a constant battle to keep the water at chemical levels that are not natural for it.

71

PART THREE

Choosing Fish

7

Some Popular Freshwater Tropical Fish

One of the most confusing things for a newcomer to tropical fish keeping is the vast number of different kinds of fish that are referred to in various publications. To compound the problem, many of these fish may be hard to find in the fish store, or may appear under completely different names.

According to Ken Strassfield, owner of "Pets Ahoy" in Norwalk, Connecticut, that's why the majority of first-time tropical fish owners opt to purchase only a few species of fish. They will almost always ask for the easily identified, well-publicized varieties—angelfish, sword-tails, platys, mollies, and catfish—thereby missing out on other species that might be more colorful, interesting, or satisfactory.

It *is* very difficult to discuss all of the different kinds of fish that are suitable for the average tropical fish keeper without adding to the confusion. What's more, new strains or varieties within strains are constantly developed through specialized breeding, or suddenly appear on the market from new sources.

Fish Classifications

Scientific classification of fish is extremely complex and seems to be subject to changes in "fashion" from time to time. Here are some of the commonly accepted classifications of fish that are referred to in this chapter. In some instances, the names used are "family" names, and in others, they are suborders of families, but in all cases they are those that are most often used.

Anabantids (Anabantidae family) are also called labyrinth fish because they have a special extra breathing organ composed of labyrinthlike folds located just behind their gills that enables them to store atmospheric oxygen obtained from the water surface. This allows them to survive in even the poorest, oxygen-depleted waters. Most male anabantids make bubble-nests at the surface of the water in which fertilized eggs are deposited by the female and subsequently guarded by the male. The tiny fry, also looked after by their fathers, can be difficult to raise because they are so small. Anabantids are omnivorous and easy to keep because of their tolerance for all kinds of water.

Catfish See *page 84.*

Characins (Characidae family) and characin-related fish have an adipose fin and/or sharp, well-developed teeth. They are generally hardy and easy to care for and most can live in slightly acid, soft tap water. They are omnivorous or carnivorous. Small schooling characins are good citizens in community tanks.

Cichlids (Cichlidae family) are an extremely large and varied group of fish, characterized by several common physical and behavioral traits. All cichlids have a single dorsal fin (the spiny and soft portions of the fin are joined in one structure), a single pair of nostrils, and an incomplete, or broken, lateral line. They are intelligent, and all engage in some form of advanced parental care of their eggs and young and are territorial and aggressive when breeding. All cichlids produce a lot of waste and particular care must be given to maintain good water quality. Almost all cichlids are predatory and will eat any fish that is small enough.

Cyprinids (Cyprinidae family) are a large, colorful family with a wide variety of life styles. Their common characteristics are the lack of an adipose fin and no teeth in their jaws. Instead, they have teeth in their throats (pharyngeal teeth) to grind up their food. Most are easy to keep and are happiest in schools or groups. Cyprinids contain so-called "alarm cells" in their skin that give off a warning odor to their schoolmates if they are damaged. They are omnivorous.

Killifish   see *page 96*

Livebearers, or livebearing fish, come from many different families. Their common denominator is that their eggs are fertilized and hatched within the female, and fry are fully formed at birth. Male livebearers have modified tube-like rays on their anal fins with which they deposit sperm into the females' cloaca. Most are omnivorous, with a preference for algae and greens.

Loaches   see *page 98*

Some Tropical Freshwater Fish

Fish in this section are listed under their popular, non-scientific name or in familiarly named groups with common characteristics.

African Lake Cichlids

The cichlids that come from Lake Malawi and Lake Tanganyika in East Africa are used to living in habitats that

77

contain plenty of rocks and caves that provide cover for hiding, breeding, and raising young. The lakes' water is quite hard, as it contains lots of minerals from the mountain streams that feed them.

Lake cichlids are generally quite active, constantly on the move while grazing among the rocks to gather algae. Generally, they swim where the rocks are—in the middle to lower levels of the water. They are voracious eaters, and will tear apart any natural plants that are in the aquarium.

They are usually quarrelsome and territorial, especially when breeding, during which time pairs will set up residence in rocky nooks, crannies, and caves. All lake cichlids should be kept in species-specific tanks, in tanks with other same-size cichlids, or with small, peaceful schooling fish known as "dither" fish, that can swim fast and will provide distraction and security for the cichlids.

Enough space should be provided so that each breeding pair or harem group can set up its own territory without encroaching on other pairs or groups.

Two interesting and distinct forms of breeding occur among these fish. The egg depositors, like the julies, lay their eggs in the recesses of caves. They are what is known as harem-brooders—that is, one male will mate with several females. The eggs and young may be guarded and tended by the male or by both parents.

Mouth-breeders, such as Fuelleborn's cichlids, pair off into couples. After the eggs are laid by the female, they are fertilized by the male in various ways, and the female then incubates the eggs in her throat for about three weeks. In a few species, the male incubates the eggs.

African lake cichlids are found in a wide variety of colors and can be very difficult to sex when young. As they mature the males are generally larger, have longer fins, and are more colorful, especially at breeding time.

They eat all foods, but are especially fond of vegetation and algae, the growth of which should be encouraged. Because they are voluminous eaters, they produce a lot of waste which is not broken down in the hard water. Therefore, they require frequent water changes.

Summary

Fish size: From 2 to 4+ inches

Behavior: Lively, aggressive, and territorial; usually inhabit the middle and lower levels of an aquarium; will eat plants and may dig them up

Tank: Large; species-specific or like species

Furnishings: Lots of rocks and retreats; very hardy plants, if any

Light: Good light for algae growth; floating plants for shade and fry hiding places

Water: Temperature around 75°; alkaline (pH 8 or over); medium hard to hard; frequent changes

Food: Omnivorous/variety; lots of algae and green food

Angelfish

Angelfish are also cichlids (see *pages 77-79*), but they come from South American rivers where the water is somewhat acidic and soft. These beautiful disc-shaped fish like to slip between reeds and grasses near the riverbanks and need similar cover in an aquarium or they may become nervous and skittish. They do not eat or uproot plants. A deep tank provides the best environment for the kinds of plants that angelfish like.

At the same time, they should have plenty of open space for swimming. Although angelfish are slow-moving, their compressed body shape, large, erect dorsal and anal fins, and long, flowing ventral fins and tail rays, mean that they need room in order to swim freely.

Angelfish are generally peaceful and school when young. As they mature, they will usually pair off. There are no color or size differences between males and females, making sexing difficult. To a practiced eye, the females appear to bulge somewhat underneath their pectoral fins and have a fatter-appearing breeding tube.

Although they can be kept in a community tank with other slow-moving fish, angelfish will become nervous if they are constantly forced to get out of the way of very active fish, and will fare better in a species-specific aquarium. When an angelfish is nervous or upset, it will become pale and colorless. Although they may be frightened of people at first, they will often become very tame when settled in.

Breeding pairs may be territorial. As all cichlids do, angelfish take very good care of their young. Eggs are laid in the open, and both parents fan the eggs continuously with their fins in order to keep fresh water flowing over them. When the eggs hatch, they are carried in the parents' mouths to plants, where they hang suspended from a sticky thread until they drop to the bottom where the parents have prepared a sand area for them. After about four days, the fry become free-swimming, but are guarded by their parents for eight to ten weeks.

Traditionally, angelfish are silvery-colored with vertical black stripes, pale blue tips on their ventral fins, and red spots in their eyes. New strains have been developed in various combinations of black and all black. If they have

enough space, angelfish can grow to be six inches long and
ten inches high, including fins.

Summary

Fish size: Average 4 to 5 inches around

Behavior: Peaceful; slow, graceful swimmers; midwater swimmers and feeders; may become tame

Tank: Large, deep; plenty of swimming space; can be kept with other peaceful fish, but fare best in species-specific tank

Furnishings: Tall, reedlike plants for cover

Light: Subdued

Water: Temperature 72° to 78°—higher for breeding; slightly acidic (pH 7 or less); soft

Food: All kinds of live food

Barbs

Barbs are cyprinids. They usually have several barbels,
or whiskerlike protrusions, at the corners of their mouths
that help them to locate food.

Although there are barbs that reach seven inches in size,
the popular aquarium varieties are usually small (under three
inches at maturity), active, schooling fish. The Asian waters in which they are found are generally well-vegetated,
large in area, and quietly flowing, with a lot of open surface
area, so barbs like a lot of swimming area with plenty of
plants on the peripheries.

Most barbs are schooling fish and some, like the tiger barb,
will become very unhappy if they do not have some other
family members around. Their unhappiness can cause

sulking, anorexia, and aggressive behavior toward other fish in the tank. Tiger barbs have a reputation for fin-nipping other fish, but experienced aquarists have found that keeping them in small schools cuts down or prevents this behavior.

Barbs are lively and very active at all levels of the tank. They are generally peaceful and can be kept in a community tank with other peaceful fish as long as there is plenty of space.

Depending on the type of barb, the males are usually easily distinguished from the females by a different body shape and brighter coloration. Although most barbs spawn readily they tend to eat their own eggs.

Summary

Fish size:	Most commonly kept aquarium varieties—under 3 inches
Behavior:	Lively, active; generally peaceful, schooling; most are bottom-feeders
Tank:	Large enough to provide plenty of surface and swimming space; community tank with other peaceful fish
Furnishings:	At least 2 to 3 plantings; some floating plants
Light:	Good light; some need shade or subdued light
Water:	Temperature average 75°—higher for breeding. Neutral (pH 7 or so); soft to medium-hard
Food:	Omnivorous—good eaters; all foods

Bettas

Betta splendens, or Siamese fighting fish, are anabantids.

Bettas have been selectively bred to achieve their present striking appearance. Males are brightly colored in a wide variety of hues and have long, flowing tails, anal and dorsal fins, and long pointed ventral fins.

Although they are slow-moving and peaceful with other kinds of fish, male bettas will fight each other to the finish. When two males meet their color will heighten, they will spread their fins stiffly and extend their gill covers until they look like ruffs around their necks before beginning to fight. During a fight the fish will tear each other's fins until one of them is no longer able to maneuver at all. A male betta will even "attack" his own image in a mirror!

Because of their aggressiveness, two males can never be kept in the same tank, but several females can be peacefully kept with one male.

Summary

Fish size: Up to 2.5 inches

Behavior: Slow-moving; surface-feeders; males highly aggressive with each other

Tank: Size is not significant, but there should be plenty of surface area, single males are often kept in very small bowls; can be kept in community aquarium with other kinds of fish; good cover to prevent jumping out and to keep water surface warm

Furnishings: Plants

Light: Level not especially important—moderate

Water: Temperature around 75°—higher for breeding; other factors not particularly significant

Food: All foods, mostly live

Catfish

There are several different families of catfish that are normally kept in home aquariums. As a group, they share several characteristics. Catfish have well-developed Weberian apparatuses (see *Chapter One*). They do not have scales, but some, like the popular South American corydoras catfish, also called dwarf armored catfish (bronze, leopard, black-spotted, peppered), have armored "plates" instead. Sucking catfish, such as the plecos, have no plates on their stomachs, while other catfish are completely naked. All catfish have barbels that help them to find food on the bottom, but some are predatory and feed at all levels.

Because they are so diverse, it is difficult to generalize about catfish. Most of the types found for sale in fish stores are peaceful and will do well in a community tank, but should be kept with other fish that are the same size or larger than they are.

All catfish, whether or not they are in the nocturnal majority, require some hiding places in an aquarium. Care must be taken not to inadvertently leave a space in which a catfish might become trapped in its effort to hide. Pieces of equipment or inflexible tank furnishings should be firmly attached to the aquarium glass or bottom so that a fish can't become stuck behind or beneath them. Because many catfish graze on the bottom and may also dig small excavations in which to bury themselves, the gravel should not have any sharp edges.

Although most catfish are omnivorous scavengers and will eat other fish's leftovers, they must be provided with their own food which will fall to the lower levels of the aquarium. If top and middle-level swimmers grab all of the food before it gets to the bottom, your catfish will soon go hungry!

Summary

Fish size: Dwarfs and small upside-down catfish don't exceed 3 inches; suckermouths may grow to 9 or 10 inches; glass—up to 4 inches; banjo—up to 6 inches

Behavior: Many are gregarious and need company; most are active at night; most swim and feed at lower levels, except for glass and upside-down

Tank: Smaller catfish are suitable for community tanks with other same-sized or larger fish; suckermouths may suck on other fish, and naked and bagrid catfish are predatory toward smaller fish

Furnishings: Sandy bottom; hiding-places—see precautions above

Light: No special requirements

Water: Temperature around 75°; dwarf armored—no higher than 75°; no special requirements as to pH

Food: Most are omnivorous, but favor algae and greens; care should be taken that food is available to all fish

Danios

Danios are peaceful, swiftly active cyprinids that generally inhabit fast-flowing, cool waters. They are schooling fish that thrive in the company of their kind.

Used to feeding at the surface in the wild, danios are characterized by flat backs, upturned mouths, and dorsal fins that are fairly far back on their bodies. They like a lot of light, are not skittish, and may jump out of the water given the opportunity.

The most common danio is the tiny zebra from India.

85

Summary

Fish size: Most are under 2.5 inches, except the giant danio, which can be 4+ inches long

Behavior: Very lively, active; peaceful; keep in school group; surface-swimmer/feeder; jumper

Tank: Large, shallow, long; plenty of swimming space; community tank; cover to prevent jumping out

Furnishings: Lots of plants

Light: Ample light/sun

Water: Temperature should be cool—under 75° except for breeding; no special pH or hardness requirements, but need lots of fresh water regularly; good aeration

Food: Omnivorous; easy to feed

Discus Fish

Discus fish, or Pompadour fish, are beautiful, delicate cichlids that inhabit the gently flowing waters at the edges of the Amazon River basin where there are lots of hiding-places and the light is filtered through vegetation. They are apt to be shy and easily stressed.

Considered to be among the most difficult of aquarium fish to keep successfully, discus fish require very specific water conditions in order to thrive. They are also highly susceptible to protozoan and bacterial diseases that can be carried by other seemingly healthy fish (and even some live foods) and are best kept in a species-specific tank.

Another reason for keeping discus in a species tank is that they can be very aggressive and territorial when they reach maturity and pair off for breeding. There are no clearly visible sexual differences, and aquarists usually allow their discus to choose their own mates from the school. Adult discus need a large enough tank so that each pair can stake out a territory. Ideally, once a pair is ready to breed it should have an entire tank to itself. Like their cousins, the angelfish, they are excellent parents, guarding and fanning their eggs from the time that they are laid. Discus fish are unusual in that the young actually eat mucus secreted from their parents' bodies.

Many different colors have been developed through selective breeding.

Summary

Fish size: Up to 6 inches on average

Behavior: Slow-swimming at all levels; schooling when young, then pairing off; peaceful but territorial and aggressive when guarding young; apt to be skittish

Tank: Large, deep; species-specific

Furnishings: Hiding places; surfaces for egg-depositing (e.g., rocks, clay flowerpots, tiles); floating plants

Light: Subdued

Water: Temperature 82° or more; acid (pH 6.5 or lower); very soft, fresh; good filtration

Food: High-quality meaty food—be very careful of contamination; some plant food

Dwarf Cichlids

The term "dwarf cichlids" is used to describe the size of the fish, and dwarf cichlids differ in their origins and environmental needs.

South American dwarfs such as the ram and checkerboard cichlids and the Kribensis or dwarf rainbow from West Africa require soft, slightly acidic water, for instance. Those from the African lakes (see *pages 77–79*) thrive in hard water.

All dwarf cichlids are schooling, and active, and are apt to be shy and skittish. They benefit from the presence of dither fish in the aquarium (see *African Lake Cichlids, pages 77–79*). Like the lake cichlids, they require plenty of cover and hiding-places and are apt to be spooked by too much light from above so that floating plants are very important.

Summary

Fish size:	Most under 3 inches at maturity
Behavior:	Schooling; lively; apt to be shy
Tank:	Plenty of space per fish; species-specific; dither fish recommended
Furnishings:	Lots of cover; floating plants and rocks, depending on species
Light:	Subdued
Water:	Water quality very important; chemistry depends on species
Food:	Omnivorous

Gouramis

Like bettas (see *page 83*), gouramis are also anabantids, or labyrinth fish, and share their breathing and bubble-nest-building traits (except for the kissing gourami which does not build a bubble-nest). They are also able to survive in very poor water conditions.

Unlike bettas, gouramis are not fierce fighters. They are generally slow-moving, shy, and peaceful, although they may become territorial when breeding. Mature males can be differentiated from females by their darker, brighter colors at breeding time.

Gouramis range in size from the tiny honey gourami, which is under two inches long at maturity, to the large kissing gourami, which can grow up to eight or more inches long. Most have elongated ventral fins with taste cells at the tips that look and act like feelers. They can move these fins around in all directions to help them locate food.

Kissing gouramis are probably the best known because of their interesting habit of seeming to "kiss" each other with their lips puckered. There are many theories as to why they do this, but the primary use of their protruding lips is to scrape algae off of surfaces with their rasping edges. Kissing gouramis sometimes suck on other fish in the aquarium.

Summary

Fish size: Wide range of sizes, from under 2 inches to 6

Behavior: Slow-moving, graceful; generally peaceful; suitable
for a community tank; surface-feeder/breather

Tank: Depending on fish size, should be large and shallow; good cover to keep fish from jumping out and
to keep the surface water warm

Furnishings: Lots of plants and hiding places

Light: Medium; some shade

Water: Around 75° for most—some (*e.g.*, croaking) need
higher temperatures; neutral water

Food: Omnivorous; all foods

Guppies

Guppies, or millions fish, are the most well known of the
many kinds of livebearers.

Hardy, active, and adaptable schooling fish, guppies are
often used as "guinea pigs" by aquarists to test the waters
for more delicate species. They are also used to help control
mosquitoes in the tropics by eating the larvae.

Although they come in an enormous variety of colors and
markings, guppies are easily recognized by their upturned
mouths and enormous eyes. The tiny males are the most
colorful and have elongated fins. Females are larger and
duller-hued, but some have recently been developed with
bright-colored tails.

Choosing Fish

Guppies are peaceful with other fish, but the males may quarrel with each other during breeding time (which is almost all of the time). They are prolific breeders but may cannibalize their young.

Summary

Fish size: Males up to 1.25 inches; females up to 2 inches

Behavior: Lively; very active; surface-feeder; schooling; peaceful

Tank: Small to medium size

Furnishings: Lots of plants

Light: Bright light

Water: Around 75° or more—higher for successful breeding; neutral (pH 7 to 8); hardness not too important, but can tolerate hard water well

Food: Omnivorous; all foods—lots of variety

Halfbeaks

These very interesting little livebearing fish come from Southeast Asia. They are distinguished by their immobile, elongated lower jaws. The best known of the halfbeaks is called the wrestling halfbeak because the males often grab each other by their long beaklike jaws and twist and turn like wrestlers. Because of the males' penchant for fighting, it is best to keep these fish in groups consisting of one male and several females.

They are typical surface-dwellers and -feeders, with their flattened backs and rear-set dorsal fins, and are peaceful with fish that occupy other aquarium levels.

Halfbeaks can easily injure their jaws if they bump into the glass sides of the tank, so it's best to provide peripheral plantings.

Although they breed readily, they are cannibalistic toward their fry.

Summary

Fish size: 2.5 to 3 inches long

Behavior: Schooling; surface-swimmers/-feeders; peaceful toward other fish; males will fight with each other

Tank: Wide, shallow; good cover to prevent jumping out

Furnishings: Peripheral planting; floating plants

Light: Good light

Water: Neutral, hard water with some salt added (approx. 1 tsp. per gal.)

Food: Live only

Hatchetfish

There are two familiar types of hatchetfish, the commonly seen marbled, and the more delicate silver hatchetfish. They are closely related to characins and are usually grouped with them.

Choosing Fish

Hatchetfish are easily recognized by their straight backs, triangular, hatchet-shaped bodies, and elongated winglike pectoral fins. They are surface-swimmers and -feeders and can actually "fly" over the water's surface for some distance, using their pectoral fins to keep them aloft. A good cover is essential to keep hatchetfish from jumping out of the tank.

Naturally peaceful and somewhat shy, hatchetfish spend most of their time resting just underneath the surface of the water waiting for food to alight. They are schooling fish and several can be kept in a community tank with other fish that normally occupy lower levels of the water.

Summary

Fish size: Marbled—up to 1.75 inches; silver—up to 2 + inches

Behavior: Peaceful; may be shy at first; surface-swimmer /-feeder; will jump; schooling

Tank: Long tank preferable; good cover to keep fish from jumping out and to keep the surface water warm

Furnishings: Floating plants

Light: Shade and subdued light

Water: 75° or more; acid (pH 5.5 to 6.5); soft

Food: All floating foods, mostly live, some dried

Headstander

Just like hatchetfish, above, headstanders are also usually grouped with characins.

The spotted headstander is an attractive silvery-colored fish with red eyes that gets its name from its habit of swimming and resting in the water with its head pointed down. It can also be recognized by a square-shaped dorsal fin. Although the headstander may swim in both the middle and lower levels of the aquarium, it is a bottom-feeder.

Because headstanders naturally live among rocks in fast-moving water, the bottom of the aquarium should be dark-colored and the water needs to be kept very fresh.

Headstanders are active schooling fish and require company of their own kind. They are peaceful and nonaggressive.

Summary

Fish size: Up to 4 inches

Behavior: Schooling—need company; peaceful; active; bottom-feeders

Tank: Medium-to-large size; swimming space

Furnishings: Dark bottom; lots of plants and hiding places

Light: Subdued; shade

Water: Around 75°; slightly acid (pH 6 +); soft; good filtration

Food: All food; plenty of algae/vegetable matter

Jack Dempsey

The Jack Dempsey is a cichlid that earns its name by being extremely excitable and pugnacious. It is also destructive and will tear and uproot any plants that are in the tank.

Despite these drawbacks, Jack Dempseys are beautiful fish that become blue-black with shiny green scales when they mature. Schooling when young, they pair off into strongly mated couples at maturity. Like all cichlids, they are devoted parents.

Jack Dempseys are voracious eaters and therefore create a great deal of waste.

Summary

Fish size: Up to 7 or 8 inches

Behavior: Aggressive, pugnacious; destructive

Tank: Large, species-specific

Furnishings: No plants; coarse gravel or stones

Light: Medium

Water: Temperature around 72° to 75°; higher for breeding. Average pH and hardness; frequent water changes

Food: Mostly large, live food (*e.g.*, whole shrimp, worms; some greens; large quantity

---

Killifish

Killifish, also known as egg-laying toothcarps and top minnows, are in the cyprinodontidae family. They are usually small, very colorful fish, characterized by having teeth and the typical flat backs, far-back dorsal fins, and upturned mouths of surface swimmers. Most live in schools in well-shaded pools.

Killifish have two very distinct breeding methods. Those that come from tropical Africa, Asia, and South America inhabit pools that dry up when the rains cease. They are called "annual fish," and live for only about eight months in the wild—somewhat longer in captivity. They are prolific breeders, and bury their eggs in the mud before it dries up, where they remain viable for a long time, hatching only when the next rains come. Other species of killifish that are not dependent on the rains, such as American flagfish, hang their eggs on bushy plants. They are longer-lived than their cousins, surviving in captivity for three to four years. Sexing is easy, as the males are much brighter and have more elaborate fins than the females do.

Because most killifish require very specific water conditions, they should be kept in species-specific tanks in schools or groups. Despite their small size, many of them are quite pugnacious.

Summary

Fish size: 1.5 to 3 inches long

Behavior: Most are active; surface-swimmers/feeders; may jump; schooling; some are aggressive

Tank: Small-size tank OK; good cover to prevent jumping out; species tank

Furnishings: Hiding places; bushy plants

Light: Shaded light

Water: For many, water temperature can be low—around 70°; soft, acid, peaty, top-quality; some salt added

Food: All foods

Labeo Bicolor (Red-tailed Black Shark) and Labeo Erythrurus (Redfin Shark)

These delightful cyprinids from rivers and streams in Thailand look like small sharks. They have torpedo-shaped, flat-bottomed bodies and their mouths, which are situated underneath their snouts, have two pairs of barbels.

They are moderately active mid- and lower-level swimmers, feed on the bottom, but may turn upside-down in order to graze on algae. Bicolors in particular are playful and indulge in various antics. Sometimes they will frighten their owners by resting on their sides at the bottom of the tank. Although they may be territorial and quarrelsome with their own kind, they are peaceful and compatible with other fish.

97

Summary

Fish size: Up to 4.75 inches

Behavior: Moderately active; playful; may be territorial with other labeos; bottom-feeder/algae grazer

Tank: Large

Furnishings: Lots of plants and hiding places

Light: Subdued/moderate

Water: Temperature around 75°—not too warm; alkaline (pH 7.4); soft

Food: All foods; algae

Loaches and Botias

Botias are usually grouped with loaches. Both are members of the cobitidae family. Like catfish, loaches are scaleless bottom-dwellers and often burrow into the sand. They are equipped with barbels and well-developed lips with raspy surfaces that help them to find and gather algae and other food in the often muddy bottom waters. Coolie and chain loaches each have three pairs of barbels, while clowns have four! Loaches don't breathe through their mouths but through the upper part of divided gill openings. This allows them to hang onto a surface without having to let go to breathe.

Their body shapes are varied. Some, for example, coolies, are wormlike, while others have flat bottoms and arched backs. Some loaches are very sensitive to changes in barometric pressure, earning them the name "weather loaches." They are generally shy, peaceful, and gregarious and need to be kept in groups or they will be very unhappy. Most are nocturnal, but the tiny chain or dwarf loach may be active in the daytime.

Because they are quite active and fast-moving, loaches are apt to stir up any debris that hasn't been cleaned from the bottom of the tank.

Summary

Fish size:	Ranges from the tiny chain at 1.25 inches, up to 5 inches
Behavior:	Lively; most nocturnal; bottom-dweller, burrower; peaceful; gregarious—need companionship
Tank:	Medium
Furnishings:	Plants; deep layer of soft sand; rocks and hiding places
Light:	Subdued at bottom of tank
Water:	75° and up; fresh; neutral; soft
Food:	All foods, especially worms

Mollies

Mollies are very popular livebearing fish that have been developed in various new strains, fin and tail shapes, and colors, the most common of which are the black molly and the sailfin molly.

Most mollies are active, schooling fish that inhabit all

levels of an aquarium. They require a lot of space in which to swim and lots of light to encourage the growth of algae.

Given the right water conditions, mollies breed easily. The eggs are fertilized and develop internally so that live fry are born.

Mollies require warm, very hard water in order to thrive and breed and are therefore kept in a species-specific tank. They are peaceful, however, and can be maintained in a community tank as long as they are provided with a "molly block," a slow-dissolving salt tablet that can be hung on the side of the tank. In these conditions they will rarely breed successfully.

Summary

Fish size:	Average 3 to 4 inches
Behavior:	Active, schooling; swim at all levels; surface-feeder; peaceful
Tank:	Large—ample swimming space
Furnishings:	Well-planted
Light:	Lots of light to encourage algae growth
Water:	Warm—over 75°—metabolism (breeding potential) increases with temperature; alkaline (pH 7 to 8); very hard—add salt (approx. 1.5 tsp. per gal.) or use a "molly block"
Food:	Omnivorous, constant surface-feeder; plenty of vegetable matter/algae

---

Orange Chromide

The orange chromide is one of only a few species of cichlid that come from Asia.

It is a relatively nonaggressive cichlid that is not as destructive as many of its relatives and will not usually pull up sturdy plants, although it does dig pits when breeding.

Summary

Fish size: Up to 3.5 inches

Behavior: Peaceful except at breeding time; may be shy; mid- and lower-level swimmer

Tank: Large; can be kept in a community tank with similar-size fish

Furnishings: Sturdy plants; hiding places

Light: Moderate or subdued

Water: Average 75°; hard water with some sea salt added

Food: All foods

Oscar

The oscar, or velvet cichlid, is the largest of cichlids when full grown. Although it is slow-moving and fairly nonaggressive, it requires a very large aquarium. Oscars produce waste in proportion to their ravenous appetites.

Schooling when young, they form pairs when mature, but can be kept alone. An oscar may become very tame and even allow itself to be hand-fed and petted.

Summary

Fish size: Up to 14 inches

Behavior: Peaceful; destructive: digs up plants

Tank: Very large; 70 or more gallons for an adult Oscar

Furnishings: No rooted plants; rocks and deep gravel

Light: Moderate—no special requirements

Water: Temperature—average 75°; no special other requirements, but frequent changes and excellent filtration are necessary

Food: Omnivorous; very large eater

Other Cichlids

There are far too many other cichlids to mention individually. They vary in origin, habitat, size, water requirements, and aggressiveness/compatibility with other fish.

Some, such as the smallish (up to 4 inches) South American keyhole cichlid, and two larger species from Central America, the firemouth cichlid and the festive cichlid, which is a rivermate of the angelfish, are relatively peaceful with other fish except in spawning time. Others, for example, the four-inch convict (zebra) cichlid from Central America, are highly aggressive at all times and must be kept in a species-specific tank.

All are excellent parents and take care of their fry until they are able to fend for themselves.

Pencilfish

These slim, torpedo-shaped fish are characinlike, as are hatchetfish and headstanders.

The best-known are the three-banded and one-line pencilfish that change color dramatically at night for better camouflage. Pencilfish are lively, alternately resting and darting about the upper levels of the tank. They usually live in schools in gently flowing shallow streams and are peaceful and nonaggressive with other fish.

Summary

Fish size: Up to 2.75 inches

Behavior: Peaceful; schooling; lively

Tank: Small to medium; good cover to prevent jumping out; keep with other small fish

Furnishings: Lots of plants

Light: Good light

Water: 75° and up; soft, medium acidity

Food: All small foods; live foods; surface-feeder

Piranhas

There are sixteen species of piranhas, generally grouped with characins. Red-bellied piranhas are the type most often kept in home aquariums. These meat-eating fish, with their large, interlocking, pointed teeth, have a bad reputation for aggressiveness and will, indeed, attack if they smell blood. The ferociousness of the attack is generally related to the size of the school. Usually, only young, partially grown individuals are kept in home fish tanks. They swim in schools and are predatory to other fish, no matter how large.

Piranhas come from the flowing waters of the Amazon River basins where they swim at all levels.

Summary

Fish size: Up to a foot or more

Behavior: Schooling; very aggressive and predatory; may be shy in an aquarium; generally slow-moving and quiet; inhabits all tank levels

Tank: Large, with lots of swimming space

Furnishings: Hardy plants; moderate planting

Light: Moderate

Water: Average temperature 75°; soft to medium-hard, slightly acid water

Food: High-protein, meaty food

Platys

Platys are hardy, lively, peaceful livebearing fish from Central America. Many colors and color combinations have been developed through selective breeding.

They are naturally schooling fish and should be kept in groups. They swim and eat at all water levels. They are prolific breeders.

═══════════════════════════════════════

Summary

Fish size: Up to 2.75 inches

Behavior: Lively, "cheerful," peaceful; schooling; feed and swim at all levels

Tank: Small to medium, depending on number of fish

Furnishings: Dark, sandy bottom material; good number of plants and floating plants

Light: Lots of good light

Water: Average 75°; alkaline (pH 8), medium-hard to hard; frequent changes

Food: Hearty eater; all foods; algae

═══════════════════════════════════════

Rasboras

Rasboras are a large genus of fish in the cyprinid family. There are many sizes and shapes of rasboras but all are active, peaceful, schooling fish that inhabit the upper and middle levels of an aquarium. They all require lots of swimming space.

Two well-known rasboras are the scissortail and the harlequin. Although scissortails can grow to six inches in the wild, they rarely top three inches in an aquarium. They have a typical long, slim rasbora body, and are easily identified by their forked tails that open and close like a pair of scissors as they swim. Tiny harlequins, on the other hand, have short bodies and rounded abdomens. They are also easily identified by the dark triangles at the backs of their bodies.

Summary

Fish size: Varies—most under 3 inches

Behavior: Active, schooling; thrive in groups; peaceful; upper-level swimmer

Tank: Size depends on fish size; need plenty of swimming area

Furnishings: Dark bottom material; plants

Light: Subdued

Water: Average 75°—scissortail lower temps; acidic (pH 5.3 to 6), soft to medium-hard

Food: All foods; live food

Swordtail

These livebearers from Central America have been developed in many colors and fin types. They are hardy, lively, and generally peaceful but males may bully each other. Adult males are easily distinguished by the swordlike, extended lower section of their tails.

Swordtails swim in loosely formed schools. Although

106

they are peaceful and can be kept in a community tank, their high level of activity may disturb other quieter fish. Males also have a habit of shooting backward in the water for several inches when courting, an action that is sure to startle tankmates.

They are prolific, but may eat their young.

Summary

Fish size: Males (without sword) 3.5 inches; females larger

Behavior: Extremely active; swim at all levels, but is a surface-feeder; jumps

Tank: Size can vary, but plenty of swimming space

Furnishings: Dense planting; good cover to prevent jumping

Light: Good light

Water: Cooler than average (73° or so); pH 7 to 8; hard

Food: All foods—lots of greens

Tetras

There are many kinds of tetras, which are members of the characin family. Most tetras are hardy, lively, active fish that are quite easy to keep. They are schooling fish that should be kept in groups and require plenty of swimming space.

Well-known tetras include the tiny neons, larger cardinals, and bleeding hearts.

107

Summary

Fish size: Varies considerably, from under 1 inch up to 3 inches

Behavior: Peaceful, very active; schooling

Tank: Depends on size of fish; lots of swimming space needed

Furnishings: Dark bottom; plants

Light: Moderate

Water: Varies; usually soft to medium-hard, neutral to slightly acidic

Food: All foods

And More

There are many other freshwater tropical fish that are suitable for and available to the average aquarist. As you become acquainted with the hobby you may find one or more wonderful "new" fish to add to your collection.

8

Making a Selection

It's really "putting the cart before the horse" to buy an aquarium and tank equipment before you decide what kind of fish you want to keep. Even if you know that you are going to start out simply with a small community tank, your fish selection should govern the size of your aquarium, the kind and size of filtering equipment you buy, and so forth. However, you can't actually buy your fish until you have the aquarium set up, running, and ready to go (see *Chapter Nine*).

Before you make a decision, an important part of your research should include looking at all of the fish that you can. Visit several dealers if possible, ask a lot of questions, and listen to the answers before you decide what you are going to buy. A good fish dealer will be knowledgeable and can provide you with a lot of information, but only if you ask and listen to the answers. Don't go into a store and state a lot of preconceived ideas because the clerk or owner will assume that you know what you're talking about, or may decide that you may have already made up your mind and won't try to talk you out of it, even if he thinks that you're wrong, for fear of losing your business.

A Source

The first thing that you have to do is select a dealer from whom to buy your fish. In *Chapter Three*, the advantage of buying your equipment from the same source that you purchase your fish was mentioned, but how do you choose a good fish store?

In general, a chain store is not a good source for fish unless you know exactly what you're doing. When it comes to selecting fish, the people who work in chain stores usually can't help you very much. These large stores have a hard time recruiting sufficient help and often end up with part-time students who may or may not know anything at all about fish. You may be lucky and find a salesperson who does know something one day, but when you go back, that person will probably no longer be there.

In a small privately owned store there is a good deal more consistency in help and the owner is usually there to answer any questions that the salesperson can't. An individual dealer has a lot more interest in building up a satisfied clientele that will return again and again than a chain store that relies more on drop-in sales.

If you're interested in specialty fish such as cichlids, killifish, or fancy guppies, for instance, you may want to contact a local aquarium society or specialty society to locate good sources for fish. Listings of these societies can be found in several magazines devoted to fish keeping (see *Appendix B*). Breeders who raise specialty fish will sometimes sell directly to individual collectors. They advertise in fish magazines.

JUDGING A FISH STORE

Not all privately owned fish stores are equally devoted to the health of their stock and the satisfaction of their customers. So, shop around and don't make up your mind to buy from the first store that you go into.

How can you judge a good fish store if you're new to the hobby? To make a quick and reliable test, Dr. Loiselle gives the following advice:

- First, walk up and down the aisles between the tanks and look at them. If there are a lot of sick-looking or dead fish in the tanks, walk out. If the water is unclear or yellowish-colored, it's dirty—walk out. The dealer either doesn't know how to take care of his stock properly or simply doesn't care. In either case, you don't want to buy fish from him because they won't be healthy.
- If the store passes the first test, ask some simple questions about fish, such as—"Can I keep oscars and guppies in the same tank?" or "Can I keep goldfish and tropicals in the same tank?" If the dealer says, "Yes" to either question, leave. On a little bit more sophisticated level, ask if it's all right to keep neon tetras and mollies in the same tank. Again, if the answer is yes, the dealer's more interested in taking your money than in giving you good information, and you'd do better at another store. A reliable dealer will set you straight if you have mistaken ideas. One that's not so reliable will sell you anything that you say you want.

Choosing Fish

Most freshwater tropical fish are pretty and colorful, and those that aren't brightly colored are interesting to watch.

So it's a big temptation for a first-time fish buyer to really want to have "one of each."

Not only does the size of the average aquarium make this impossible, but so do the needs of the fish. Don't forget that when you set up a fish tank you're setting up a miniature environment for living creatures that may have very different needs, so it's important to select fish that will be compatible. The old saying that you can't fool around with Mother Nature has a particular application here. Even though people do mix fish that don't belong together, the end result is that one or more of the fish are going to do badly and will probably eventually develop an illness. As Dr. Loiselle says, "If you put mollies and angelfish together, someone is going to be very unhappy."

That's because their water needs differ widely. Mollies like very hard water with some salt in it, while angelfish prefer water that is much softer. If the water is hard enough to suit the mollies, the angelfish will lose their color and be prone to bacterial diseases, but if it's soft enough to suit the angelfish, the mollies will also be pale and will probably develop ich and slime mold infections. It's far better to keep mollies with other hardwater fish.

FACTORS TO CONSIDER WHEN CHOOSING FISH

Some fish are more adaptable than others to less-than-ideal conditions. Most are fairly tolerant about the amount of light they are exposed to as long as those that prefer less light have a place in which to hide. The temperature level in a tropical fish tank is usually kept in a range that is all right for most fish. But, generally speaking, water chemistry is less easy for fish to adjust to and if you want to mix fish that have different water needs, choose those whose needs fall somewhere in the middle hardness and pH range. Then you can maintain your aquarium at a neutral level and the fish will be less stressed.

Don't forget what we talked about in *Chapter Six: Water*. If you live in an area where the water is either extremely soft or extremely hard, you should choose fish that will be happy in the water, rather than having continuously to play chemist and change the water to suit the fish.

Other factors to consider are the level in the water at which a fish normally swims and its space requirements. You probably aren't likely to purchase anything but top-level surface-feeders such as hatchetfish and halfbeaks, or only bottom-dwelling catfish and loaches. But you should think in terms of the space in your aquarium as divided roughly into levels so that you don't overcrowd one area or another inadvertently, and remember that every fish needs sufficient space in which to swim at its normal speed.

Size and degree of activity and aggression should also be taken into account when you select your fish. Slow-moving fish such as bettas, gouramis, or angelfish can be literally driven crazy if they're always being bumped into by swift-moving danios, for instance. If you're planning on mixing fish with very different activity levels, be sure that there's enough space for them to swim comfortably without getting into each others' way. The long flowing fins and tails of fancy guppies and bettas will soon become very moth-eaten-looking if these fish are housed with fast-swimming fin-nippers. Needless to say, you don't want to mix large aggressive fish with small ones that will make a good dinner. In general, it's best not to try to put any aggressive, territorial fish in a community tank. That's one reason why most cichlids are kept in species-specific aquariums (the other reason is their water requirements). Use your common sense when choosing fish of different sizes and temperaments.

Body Shapes

Some surface-swimmers have special muscles that enable them to "fly" over the water surface.

Fish with discus-shaped bodies usually live in slow-moving waters and hide in grasses and other vegetation near riverbanks.

Fish that swim at the water's surface have straight, flat backs.

Cylindrical-shaped fish usually live in midwater, often in fast-flowing currents.

Bottom-dwellers have flat-bottomed bodies.

A schooling fish such as a tetra, danio, or clown loach should never be kept alone in a community tank or it will be most unhappy and will become aggressive toward other fish. Schooling fish also look much better in numbers—always purchase three or more of them. Livebearers like company and are usually purchased in pairs.

HOW MANY FISH?

First of all, you should not plan on putting all of the fish that you select into your aquarium as soon as it's ready. You want to add fish gradually, one or two at a time, so that you don't overtax your filter; more about this in *Chapter Nine*.

Second, no matter what rule of thumb you follow, inches of fish per gallon or per square inch of surface area, always plan to begin with fewer fish than the maximum number that your tank and equipment can support. There are several reasons for this. An understocked tank is healthier and less stressful for fish and, if you're a newcomer to keeping fish and make some mistakes, there will be fewer fish to suffer and perhaps die. Also, even if you have gotten your filter used to the fish population gradually, you still want to be sure that it has sufficient capacity to support your fish. If you have selected fish that produce a lot of waste, or if you have not yet figured out exactly how much to feed your fish and there's a lot of decaying food in the tank, a small number of fish will put less strain on your filter than a large one will.

Last but not least, remember that most fish purchased from fish stores are young and will grow. Some will grow a lot. Don't get yourself into the position of having to get rid of some of your well-established fish because they have grown too big and are crowding the tank.

SNAILS

While we're on the topic of having to get rid of things, don't allow yourself to be talked into buying snails for your tank. Snails are highly regarded by some as tank-cleaners and algae-removers. But in reality, they are not essential as scavengers, do not consume fish wastes, produce large volumes of waste themselves, eat plant leaves, and compete with the fish for food once the algae is all gone. It's far more effective to control algae by reducing the light and cutting back on the number of fish.

Some snails are decorative and pretty, but the trouble with most freshwater snails is that they are really pests. They multiply rapidly and once you have one snail, you will soon have hundreds. They are very difficult to get rid of and will overrun your aquarium. Snails need hard, alkaline water to keep their shells hard and will not do well in soft water. If your water is soft, you will end up with unsightly disintegrating snail shells all over your aquarium.

Unfortunately, you often become an unwitting host to snails when eggs or tiny, almost invisible babies are introduced to your aquarium on plants, gravel, or live food. Then you have to do the best you can to control them. There are snail pesticides on the market, but they can affect the water chemistry and can be dangerous to use. What's more, you will be left with a lot of dead snails cluttering up your water. Some people use snail bait to capture snails and remove them. The best thing to do is ask your dealer for advice if you have a snail problem.

When It's Time to Make a Final Selection of Fish

Once you've decided on what kinds of fish you want to have in your aquarium, and your tank is running and biologically balanced, it's time to choose your fish.

No matter how good the dealer is or how much you trust him for advice, you and you alone should make the actual selection of individual fish that you'll take home. If you have taken the time to observe a number of fish ahead of time, you should have a pretty good idea about what a healthy individual of each species looks like. Don't be shy or embarrassed to take your time choosing your fish and to ask lots of questions. The fish dealer is there to please and to help you and, if he becomes impatient with your decision-making process, perhaps you should find another dealer.

Here's a checklist of things to look for:

• First of all, don't choose a fish from a tank in which *any* of the fish look unwell

You should reject any fish that:

• Has a hollow or sunken-looking abdomen
• Has sunken eyes
• Has bent, frayed, or ragged fins or tail
• Has spots, dots, or lumps on its skin
• Doesn't have good color—you need to know what color it should be
• Is especially tiny for its type—again, you need to know what its normal size should be
• Appears to be scratching itself or rubbing on the tank bottom or furnishings

- Doesn't seem to be able to swim or rest in an upright position, but leans or tilts to one side
- Doesn't swim around and act sociable; if it is a schooling fish, doesn't stay with its schoolmates

Don't let a dealer talk you into buying a fish with any of these signs of poor health on the guise that "it's new to the tank and will adjust once you get it home," or some such excuse. It may very well "adjust" by dying. Also, don't let yourself be talked into (or talk yourself into) buying a fish that is very expensive or very rare when you first set up your aquarium. If you really want a very special fish, wait until you're sure that your tank is really running well enough to support it before you get it.

There are also some questions that you should ask your fish dealer before deciding to buy any fish.

Be sure to find out how long the fish you're interested in has been in the store. If it has been doing well for a while, chances are that it's not harboring a disease. Then ask if the water that it's in comes from the same source as yours. If the dealer doesn't know the answer to this, it's easy enough to find out from the water company. This is important to know, because if the water in the tank that a fish is occupying is very different than yours is you may have to alter the water in your tank slightly at first so that the fish can get used to it gradually.

Ask where the fish is from—a fish farm or breeder, or is it wild-caught? If it's from a fish farm or breeder, it is better accustomed to living in an aquarium than if it was wild-caught. Most freshwater tropical fish are not wild-caught, and this question is much more significant if you're buying saltwater fish.

What, and how well, does it eat? This is something that the dealer will usually tell you, but if you purchase several different kinds of fish at the same time, you might forget to ask about varying diet preferences.

What has he observed this particular fish's behavior to be like? Is it unusually shy or aggressive, for instance? If you know how a fish has been acting in the store it will help you to recognize that it is acting normally when you get it home and may save you a frantic call to the store because you think a fish is "acting funny." Ask the dealer to tell you anything else that he has learned about this particular fish, or has observed in the past with others of the same kind. Each person who keeps fish has had different experiences and has learned different ways to deal with problems, and your dealer's insights can be a big help to you.

PART FOUR

Beginning Right

9

Setting Up Your Aquarium and Introducing the Fish

Once you've brought home an aquarium and all of the equipment and furnishings that you want to use and have them spread out on the floor or table, setting it all up may seem to be an overwhelming production.

You can make it easier and avoid time-wasting mistakes and re-dos if you take the time to plan your setting-up carefully. Some people find it helpful to write down a step-by-step procedure to be sure that they haven't forgotten anything along the way, or to take notes as the fish dealer explains the setting-up process. Sometimes, a fish dealer will have a printed instruction sheet for you to follow. How ever you decide to do it, don't just plunge headlong into putting things together or you'll probably get into difficulty.

Before You Begin

Plan to set up your aquarium and start it running when you have plenty of time for the job. It's best if you can get the whole thing put together and start it running all at once.

If you have to stop for an appreciable amount of time in the middle of setting up, dust and other pollutants can get into the tank, or you may forget just where you left off and have to go back and do something over again.

First, unwrap and look over all of the equipment that you've bought and read the instructions through quickly, just to be sure that you have everything that you need. If the directions on the pump say to "attach with a such-and-such kind of clamp," or "use a particular valve," for instance, check to be certain that you have that clamp and valve on hand.

If you haven't already done so, figure out exactly how you're going to fill the tank with water when the time comes. Do you have a long enough hose and the proper attachment to connect it to your faucet? Now's the time to check this out because, unless you have a very small tank, filling it entirely by hauling water in a pail or bucket will be a tedious, back-breaking job.

Next, wash the interior of the aquarium and everything that you are going to put into the tank with clear water or water with a little salt or household bleach in it. (Never use any kind of soap because the residue will be impossible to rinse off entirely.) Rinse thoroughly. If the aquarium glass is dirty, you can clean the outside with glass cleaner, but don't spray it directly on the glass or some of the fine mist may get inside—use a cloth dampened with cleaner. To be on the safe side, wipe the inside of the aquarium again with a clean damp cloth.

Presumably, you have already decided where you are going to locate your tank. If necessary, clear off the space and cover the adjoining surfaces and floor with newspaper to protect them from the spills that are inevitable when setting up. Place whatever padding you have decided on underneath the tank.

124

Now's the time to attach whatever backdrop you've chosen to use to the back panel of the tank while you still have easy access to it, before you put the tank in place. If you've decided to use a stick-on paper backdrop, a diorama that you've created, or whatever, put it in place, check how it looks from the front, attach it carefully, and allow the adhesive to dry before moving the tank.

When you put the aquarium in place, check to be sure that you have allowed enough space behind it and to the sides for the equipment that you've bought to fit comfortably without touching the sides or the surrounding walls. Also, allow some space in front of the tank so that it isn't right at the edge of the table or counter. If the weight of a filled aquarium isn't distributed evenly it will cause a shelf or countertop to sag eventually. You also don't want your fish tank to be situated too precariously in case someone should bump into it.

The tank needs to be level—from end to end, and from front to back. If you don't happen to have a carpenter's level handy and don't want to buy one, there is another way to check this. Put the tank in place and add water to a depth of one-half inch. With an ordinary ruler, measure the depth all around the tank at each corner. If it's not level and you're using rubber matting or polystyrene underneath the tank, you can usually adjust the level by adding or taking away a bit of padding. If the surface (or your floor) turns out to be very uneven, you'll have to put something (a block of wood, for instance) underneath one side or corner of the tank or stand to build it up. Remember that once the tank is filled with water it will be very heavy, so be sure that whatever you use will be able to withstand the weight and won't gradually become squashed down. Once the aquarium's filled with water it will be very difficult, if not impossible, to readjust the level. If you do try to move a water-filled aquarium you will risk cracking it.

At the same time that you're making these adjustments, you can begin to wash the gravel under running water. It should be rinsed until the water runs completely clear.

Setting Up

Setting up should begin at the bottom of the aquarium. If you are going to use an undergravel filter, the filter plate is the first thing that needs to be put in place. Carefully place the rinsed filter plate in the bottom of the aquarium, and make sure that it fits completely flat and snug. Depending on the filter, you may need to place a layer of netting on top to catch large pieces of debris.

Now add the washed gravel. Don't pour a large amount into the aquarium at once because it will be hard to arrange. Wet gravel will stick together. Scoop it out of the bucket or pail with a cup or your hand. You will need a minimum of two inches of gravel on top of an undergravel filter and will probably want to arrange it so that it slopes up to about four inches in depth toward the back of the aquarium. If you're not using an undergravel filter, the gravel doesn't need to be quite so deep.

If you're using a filter that needs to be packed with filtering material and activated carbon, now is the time to get it ready. Don't tamp the packing material down too much or the water won't be able to flow through it freely. Put any rinsed in-tank equipment in place now, but do not start anything up yet.

When you are locating the in-tank equipment and/or furnishings, remember not to leave any spaces that could trap a curious or shy fish between the equipment and the aquarium glass or between pieces of equipment. Anchor equipment and furnishings well and arrange them so that they either fit snugly against the glass or have plenty of room for a fish to get around them easily.

Attach the tubing and any valves or clamps to the filter and pump. In order to prevent water from back-siphoning into the pump, follow the manufacturer's instructions as to the placement of the pump in relationship to the tank, the positioning of the tubing, and the need for a valve to check the flow of water. In some instances you will need to attach a loop of the airline above the level of the water in the tank.

Next, arrange any prewashed rocks, pieces of driftwood, and other furnishings in the tank so that they look pleasing and hide in-tank equipment as much as possible. If you have drawn up a design scheme, or have one in mind, you will probably find that you have to adjust your plan a bit—things never look quite the same in actuality as they do on paper. Anchor or glue the tank furnishings in place once you're satisfied with their placement.

Now you can begin to add the water, which should neither be very hot nor very cold, but as close as possible to room temperature. There are several tricks that you can use in order to avoid disturbing the gravel too much with the water's flow: you can cover the gravel with paper, direct the water into a bowl or glass that will then overflow into the tank, aim the water at the palm of your free hand or at a rock or other furnishing to deflect the stream. If you have a very large tank, you may want to clamp the hose onto the side of the tank so that you don't have to stand there and hold it, but be very careful to keep a close eye on things as the tank fills in case the clamp slips or the tank fills up more quickly than you anticipated. No matter how tempting it might be, this is not the time to go out of the room even for a few minutes.

If you're going to position live or plastic plants, don't fill the tank all of the way up or it will overflow when you put in your hand and arm. Place the already-cleaned and trimmed plants carefully. Be sure that the roots or cuttings are secured, but be careful not to bury the crowns of rooted plants (the place where the stem or leaves join the roots) or they won't grow.

Top the aquarium off with water so that the surface is in line with tank edge. If you have determined that your water needs to be treated with a dechlorinating or chloramine agent, add it now.

Check all of the tubing and valves and plug in the equipment. Set the heater-thermostat to the desired temperature and switch on the pump and filter. If the pump doesn't seem to be working right away, there may be some air trapped in a hose. Tap the hoses gently to release any air bubbles.

Put the cover glass and the hood in place and turn on the lights. The lights should be timed to go on and off at the same time that they will when the fish are in residence. Don't be upset if the water isn't crystal clear at first. It takes a while for things to settle down in a newly set-up aquarium.

The Nitrogen Cycle

Before you begin to add fish to your aquarium, you should understand the biological workings that will be taking place in it—the nitrogen cycle. No matter what kind of fish you want to keep, freshwater or saltwater, warm or cold water, you cannot add fish to a newly set-up tank without having serious problems. You must first get the nitrifying bacteria operating.

Briefly, this is how the cycle works. Fish excrete waste products into the water in the form of ammonia. Ammonia is also produced by decaying proteins such as leftover food, decaying plants, and dead fish or snails. In nature, the volume and motion of the water dissipates these wastes, but in an enclosed aquarium they will build up rapidly. Ammonia is highly toxic to fish and must either be removed from the water or neutralized. With a biological filter, the ammonia is converted into nitrite by one set of bacteria and then the nitrite is changed into nitrate by the action of another kind of bacteria. Nitrite is just as toxic to fish as ammonia is. The higher the pH, the higher the ratio of toxic ammonia. So, in a saltwater tank, ammonia is the villain. In freshwater tanks, nitrite, which is not affected by pH levels, is almost as toxic as ammonia and can build up very fast if it is not converted into nitrate. It's usually at the beginning, when a tank is first set up, that the bacteria may not be sufficiently stabilized to handle the conversion of these compounds. Problems can also arise when a large number of fish are suddenly added to a tank. That's why Dr. Loiselle suggests that testing for nitrite as well as ammonia is most important in a freshwater tank.

Beneficial bacteria must be encouraged to grow in a freshwater tank so that they are ready to do battle as soon as you add your fish. The best medium for them to grow in is either gravel or a porous substance such as sponge. That's why biological filtering systems are recommended by many.

The nitrates that result from this biological action are not harmful to fish unless they are excessive, and are used as food by plants. Good filtration and aeration and partial water changes will keep too many nitrates from building up in an aquarium.

129

"Seasoning" an Aquarium

The best way to get an aquarium up and running with the bacteria population well established is to put one or two very hardy fish into it to provide the wastes needed for the bacteria to grow. There are several kinds of fish that make good run-in subjects because they are very tolerant of poor water conditions and won't die in an unseasoned tank. Dr. Loiselle suggests a small corydoras catfish, or a pair of platys, rosy barbs, or gouramis, depending on what kind of fish you want to end up with. Let these fish stay alone in the tank for two to three weeks before you introduce any others, and the nitrogen cycle will be well into operation.

Some people recommend running the tank without any fish in it for several weeks, but without a source of waste, it will take twice as long for the biological action to get started.

If you already have an aquarium that is up and running, you can inoculate a new tank's filter with "gunk" from the established filter, or get the new tank started with one of the sponges from a used sponge-type filter, or with some bacteria-laden gravel from the old tank. There are also liquid cultures of nitrifying bacteria that can be added to an aquarium to speed up the seasoning process. These systems are very useful when you are starting up a quarantine or hospital tank. Some people keep several hardy fish in residence in a quarantine tank. Not only will they help to keep the bacterial action going, but they'll add interest to an otherwise bare aquarium.

When to Add the Fish

Whatever you do, don't add your fish to the tank too soon. And don't add all of the fish you'll eventually want to have in your collection at once. Every time you add new fish to an aquarium, an ammonia surge will develop. If you add only one or two pairs at a time, at two-to-three week intervals, the filter's capacity to handle the ammonia will build up gradually. You can't sock any filter with a huge load of fish that will produce a lot of waste without a problem. If you do, 14 days later you will have lost most of your fish and be back for more. Of course, the second batch of fish will be OK because the water will be better by then. Some people grit their teeth and take the attitude that that's only natural, that it's "an act of God and we have to accept it—everyone does it that way." Dr. Loiselle says, "Nonsense. There's no need for that to happen. It's just a matter of having some patience."

If you plan to keep fish that are not tolerant of poor water conditions in your aquarium, it's best to add them last of all, when things are really perking in the tank.

Don't forget that, once you have several well-established fish in your aquarium and everything's going well, you will want to be careful not to introduce any diseases into the tank along with the new fish. Put any newly purchased fish into your quarantine tank for two weeks until you're sure that they're healthy. If you do this you can avoid many problems.

Acclimating the Fish

The process of being brought home from the store and plopped into a new aquarium is bound to be a traumatic one for your fish. You should do everything that you can to make it less so.

The one thing in the way of acclimation that has traditionally been recommended by most people is that you accustom the new fish to the temperature of the aquarium water by floating them on the water's surface in the plastic bag they came home in for about 15 minutes to equalize the water's temperature so that the fish aren't shocked. (If you put a fish that's been in cold water into warm water too quickly it will probably die of shock. If you put one that's been in warm water into cold water, it will *certainly* die of shock.) If that's all you do, you will have prevented one kind of shock to the fish's system, but what about the quality of the water—things such as pH and hardness? If the water it's in differs from your aquarium water in these respects, the fish will also be greatly stressed.

Brian Morris tells of an acclimating system that's used by people who import expensive fish from overseas. They put the newly arrived fish in a small amount of their own water in a bucket with an airstone running in it. They put the bucket on the floor underneath the aquarium, run a drip hose down from the aquarium for an hour or two, and let the bucket gradually fill up with water from the tank so that the fish can become used to it gradually.

You can accomplish the same thing if you float the fish you've brought from the store on the aquarium's surface in a plastic container or open-topped plastic bag, and gradually add water a little at a time from the tank until the container sinks and the fish swim out of it. If you want, you can purchase a special small tank designed specifically for this purpose that allows aquarium water to gradually seep into it as it floats on the surface.

If you're planning on keeping fish that are especially territorial by nature, it's best to put them in the tank last, after all of the other fish have become well-established. If you put them in first, they'll perceive all of the other fish you introduce as "intruders" into their exclusive territory.

Daniel F. Bebak, curator of Mote Marine Science Lab-

Two Ways to Acclimate Fish to the Water in Your Aquarium

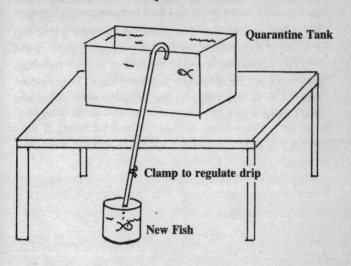

Quarantine Tank

Clamp to regulate drip

New Fish

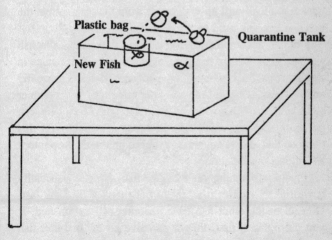

Plastic bag

New Fish

Quarantine Tank

oratory, gives this advice, ''Both marine and freshwater fish can be very territorial, and the minute you put a new fish in an aquarium, it's just like the new kid on the block—it will get picked on. We find that when we introduce a new fish it's best to do it just before the lights are going to be turned off. The original occupants of the tank go to sleep and when they wake up, the newcomer is already there. They have no time to think about it, and they usually settle down and don't make a fuss.''

10

Feeding Fish

As soon as you have any fish in your aquarium, you will have to begin to feed them. One thing that must be said at the very beginning of this chapter that will be repeated is: the number one rule for feeding fish is **DON'T OVER-FEED**. As discussed in *Chapter Nine*, decaying, uneaten food is one of the primary contributors of excessive ammonia in an aquarium. Overfeeding is one of the most common errors in fish keeping, and it can be an expensive mistake because it is one of the primary causes of fish death. In Dr. Stoskopf's opinion, "It's much easier to kill fish with kindness (overfeeding) than by starvation."

Fish have very simple, short digestive systems and do not store food in their bodies. Therefore they must eat frequently. In the wild they spend most of their time hunting for food, and they will continue with this inherent behavior in an aquarium, even though they are well fed. This is one of the reasons that first-time owners often overfeed their fish—because they "look hungry" all of the time.

Nutritional Requirements

We are all aware of the importance of proper nutrition for ourselves and out pets that are mammals, but sometimes forget that fish are living creatures, too, that have particular nutritional requirements.

It's important to find out from your dealer what kind of food or foods the fish that you buy will eat. Not all fish need the same foods. Some are carnivores (meat-eaters), some are herbivores (plant-eaters), but most are omnivores and consume a number of different kinds of food in the wild. Highly exotic fish may require a very specialized diet. Improper feeding will result in more than unhappy fish, it will create stress that can actually make a fish sicken and die.

Dr. Scott B. Citino[1] states that there has not been much research into the nutritional needs of ornamental fish kept in aquariums, but extensive research has been done on the nutritional requirements of channel catfish and members of the salmon family, which can serve as a guideline. He goes on to say that dietary deficiencies will show up more quickly and rapidly in growing fry than in adult fish, and that if fish do not breed well it may be because of improper nutrition.

Just as all other vertebrates do, fish require certain elements in their diets: proteins and some essential amino acids (the "building blocks" of protein: see *Table 1*) are for fuel and cell and tissue replacement. They are contained in all meat and fish, including live insects, crustaceans, and worms. Carbohydrates are required for energy, and are

[1]Scott B. Citino, DVM, "Providing Veterinary Care to the Commercial Fish Farmer," *The Veterinary Clinics of North America, Small Animal Practice,* Volume 18/Number 2, March 1988. Tropical Fish Medicine, Michael K. Stoskopf, DVM, PhD, Guest Editor. Philadelphia: W.B. Saunders Company.

Table 1: Essential Amino Acids and Vitamins Required by Many Fish[*]

Essential Amino Acids

Arginine
Histidine
Isoleucine
Leucine
Lysine
Methionine plus cystine
Phenylalanine plus tyrosine
Threonine
Tryptophan
Valine

Essential Vitamins

A
D
E
K
Thiamine (B1)
Riboflavin (B2)
Pyridoxine (B6)
D-calcium pantothenate
Niacin (B-complex)
Folacin (B-complex)
B-12
Inositol
Biotin (B-complex)
Choline
Ascorbic acid (C)

[*]Requirements of the substances vary between species; all are not required by every species.

Adapted from: Scott B. Citino, DVM, "Providing Veterinary Care to the Commercial Fish Farmer, "*The Veterinary Clinics of North America, Small Animal Practice,* Volume 18/Number 2, March 1988, p. 463. Tropical Fish Medicine, Michael K. Stoskopf, DVM, phD, Guest Editor. Philadelphia: W.B. Saunders Company.

available in potatoes, grain, and cereals. Vitamins and minerals (including trace elements) give a fish strong muscles, bones, and teeth, healthy nervous and circulation systems, and aid it in resisting disease. Vitamin A is found in shellfish, meat, cheese, egg yolk, seaweed, and greens. The B-complex vitamins are in green foods, including seaweed and algae, cheese, grains, and the flesh of fish and beef, beef liver, eggs, and yeast. Vitamin C is contained in seaweed, algae and other greens, beef liver, and fish roe, while Vitamin D is in algae, worms, daphnia, and shrimp. Vitamin E can be found in greens and algae, egg yolk, and grains, and Vitamin K is in greens, beef liver, daphnia, and shrimp. Most minerals can be absorbed by fish from the water, but they "cannot obtain adequate phosphorous from water absorption.[1]" Although some fat (about 10 percent of the diet) is needed, too much should be avoided, as it will foul the water.

Fortunately, most of these requirements are easy to meet if you feed your fish a good variety of foods. There are a number of different kinds of foods that can be fed to fish. Most people recommend giving fish a variety of these different kinds on a regular basis.

If yours is a community tank, housing different kinds of fish, you may have to feed quite a varied combination of foods in order to meet all of your fish's needs, and you will have to be especially careful to be sure that each fish gets its fair share of food. Feeding your fish is much easier when you have a species-specific aquarium.

Packaged and Manufactured Foods

There are a number of dry manufactured foods on the market for fish in several different forms: flakes, pellets, tablets, and granular. They are available in different sizes (very fine, fine, coarse) and different formulas, designed for different kinds of fish. They are comparable to dry foods that are made for other animals—dogs, cats, birds, guinea pigs, and so forth—in that they are made up of a balance of a number of ingredients plus vitamins and minerals designed to meet the specific nutrient requirements of fish to form a good, basic diet. They are usually packaged in tightly sealed containers and are easy to keep fresh. In general, they are a good staple diet and should make up part of your fish's food every day. One problem with dried foods is that if they are not eaten, they will sink to the bottom where they are very hard to see and will soon disappear into the gravel where they will decompose and cause bacteria to multiply.

The forms of dry manufactured food are:

- *Flakes* are made in formulas for fish that are carnivores, herbivores, or omnivores. The flakes start off floating on the surface and then sink when they become waterlogged, so are suitable for surface and midwater feeders and are best for small fish.
- *Pellets* are made in various formulas for different kinds of fish. Some pellets are made to float for surface-feeders. Others sink right away to provide food for lower-level and bottom-feeders. Pellets are better for large fish than flakes because they hold together better in the water.
- *Tablets* are made in two forms. Some are designed to be dropped into the water where they will sink to the bottom; others can be stuck to the glass so that fish can feed on them at different water levels. They too are formulated to meet different nutritional requirements.

Fresh/Live Foods

Although fish can survive on dry food alone, and many do, most are better off with at least occasional feedings of fresh, live and green food. Many aquarists feed their fish one serving of fresh (not dry) food in one form or another every day.

Live foods can be collected, grown at home, or bought, either frozen or freeze-dried. You should be aware that fresh live food, whether collected or bought, always carries the danger of contamination with it. Bacteria, protozoans, and amoebae can all be present on live foods. The risk is lessened if you know the source of the live food that you feed your fish, but some people who keep fish that are very susceptible to disease choose never to give live foods to their fish. They make up special diets instead (see *page 143*).

GREEN FOOD

For the herbivorous fish in your aquarium and the omnivores that really enjoy plants such as characins and many cichlids, algae is the best of green foods, but often there is not enough algae in the tank and you will need to supplement with fresh, well-washed, and chopped pieces of lettuce or spinach. Canned or frozen green vegetables, such as peas (squashed), are also relished by some fish.

COLLECTED LIVE FOOD

In the wild, fish naturally will hunt and eat any living organism that lights on the surface of the water, swims in the water, or lives on the bottom. It used to be a perfectly acceptable practice for fish keepers to collect various kinds of larvae, water fleas, and worms, both aquatic and nonaquatic, to feed to their fish. Unfortunately, nowadays ever-present pollution from chemical sources, insecticides, or fertilizers make feeding collected live foods very risky.

Pollution and its dangers aside, it's very easy to introduce disease into an aquarium via wild-collected live food. Parasites are usually present in all of these organisms and it's generally accepted that the dangers of feeding these foods to your fish far outweigh any possible benefits.

STORE-BOUGHT LIVE FOODS

There are several kinds of live foods that are raised specifically as fish food and are relatively free of contamination and disease organisms. They are sold in fish stores.

Daphnia, or "water fleas," are small freshwater crustaceans that are high in protein. They are well liked by fish and very popular with fish keepers. However, there is precious little "meat" inside their shells, and most fish spit out the shells, creating a lot of waste. You must be careful not to feed your fish more daphnia than can be eaten all at once because these little crustaceans will grow and take up valuable oxygen and nutrients from the water. Daphnia is also a possible source of hydra, predatory insect larvae, and protozoan parasites.

Rotifers, minute multicellular aquatic organisms, are also enjoyed by fish but they, too, can create a lot of waste in an aquarium.

Brine shrimp are used as fry food, but are also enjoyed by adult fish. They are very safe to feed. Because they live in water that's very salty, any protozoans or other disease organisms that might be present in them will die on contact with the freshwater. Frozen (as opposed to freeze-dried) brine shrimp lose most of their nutritional value. Frozen bloodworms, on the other hand, are very close to the natural food that small tropical species eat in nature, and frozen plankton and mysids are excellent for larger fish, according to Dr. Loiselle.

Tubifex worms are very popular with some fish keepers. They are red worms that live in filthy, sewage-polluted waters and must be washed thoroughly before being put into your aquarium. They are often given to fish in a special worm dispenser that either floats on the surface or is attached to the side of the aquarium with a suction cup. Tubifex worms are inexpensive and fish enjoy them, but if any are not eaten they will burrow in the gravel and die, causing serious tank pollution. Dr. Loiselle feels that there is a high correlation between the feeding of tubifex worms and the regular appearance of internal bacterial infections in fish. In his opinion it is not worth the risk of infection to feed tubifex worms, especially to long-lived fish.

Various kinds of larvae, especially, mosquito larvae, are occasionally sold in fish stores. They make excellent food and, because they are not aquatic, they won't deplete the oxygen in the tank.

Quick-freezing live food will kill most of the parasites in it (see *page 143*).

One last kind of live food is feeder fish. Large carnivorous fish such as oscars, for example, are often fed small live fish. If you are going to feed live fish, be sure that they are just as healthy as the fish you are feeding them to.

CULTURED LIVE FOODS

Some people enjoy growing live foods at home. Earthworms, white worms, and brine shrimp eggs, for example, can be hatched at home in appropriate-sized batches to provide disease-free fresh food for your fish. If stored carefully, brine shrimp eggs can last for a long time. Before feeding, any food should be rinsed thoroughly.

FREEZE-DRIED LIVE FOOD

Worms of all sorts, brine shrimp, daphnia, mosquito larvae, and a number of other live foods are now available in freeze-dried form. These foods are just as nutritious as they were before processing, can be stored indefinitely, and are free of disease organisms. Their major drawback is that they are very lightweight, and will float on the surface of the water for a long time, thereby being out of the reach of midwater and lower-level feeders. There are two solutions to this—the pieces of food can be placed in a weighted container, or they can be soaked in water before feeding.

Home-Prepared Diets

Leftover human food can be used as excellent supplemental feedings for fish. Raw lean meat, lettuce, cooked vegetables and potatoes, bits of fresh raw fish, cheese, wheat germ, and cereal flakes in small quantities are enjoyed by most fish. Don't give too much at once, and be sure to remove any uneaten food from the aquarium.

Some people go one step further and prepare their own homemade diets for their fish. A formula of raw organ meats, grains, vegetables, and appropriate supplementary vitamins and minerals can be prepared and frozen in serving-size portions. This kind of food is very polluting to water, and special care must be taken to be sure that it is all consumed quickly.

When and How Much to Feed

Several things need to be considered when feeding your fish. If you have a mixed community of fish, some are undoubtedly surface-feeders, some midwater feeders, and some bottom-feeders. Of course, small and large fish require different sizes of food. You may also have a few nocturnal fish in your collection. You have to be sure that each one of your fish gets enough food to eat and that you're not starving one individual while overfeeding another. Young, growing fish need more food than adults, and very active swimmers require more calories than slow movers do. Some fish are naturally slow, picky eaters while others quickly down their food.

It's important to be sure that all of the food that you feed your fish at each feeding is consumed in order to avoid fouling of the water. Daniel F. Bebak points out: "It's good to remember that generally a fish's stomach is no bigger than its eye." Fish should only be fed what they will eat in five minutes, and any leftover food should be immediately removed.

The best way to keep your fish eager to eat is to feed them small amounts of food several times a day. There's no hard and fast rule as to when you should feed them. Whenever it's convenient for you is fine, but be consistent and be sure that other family members know when feeding time is so that the fish are not inadvertently fed multiple times by different people. Only give the fish what they can eat up completely. "Less, more often" is a good rule of thumb. The most convenient schedule for most people is to feed their fish once in the morning and again at night. Until you're sure of the proper amount to feed each time, *watch* your fish as they eat. Don't throw the food into the tank and walk away—that's a common mistake—because if you do, you'll never know how much uneaten food is floating down to the bottom of the tank to decay. Uneaten food should be removed with a siphon immediately, before it can work its way into the gravel where it will be impossible to find and pick up.

Remember, fish in their natural habitats eat a wide variety of whatever food is available, and they always have to poke around and search for it constantly. This inborn habit of continuously poking around for food even when they are completely full leads some owners to think that their fish aren't getting enough to eat. An overfed fish will take food into its mouth out of habit, but will spit it right back out again.

A hungry fish is a healthy fish and watching your fish as they eat can also provide you with important information about them. If a formerly avid eater seems to be off its feed, it's probably sick (see *Chapter Twelve*).

CATERING TO DIFFERENT NEEDS

If you feed your fish several times a day, you can vary their diet by giving dry food at one feeding and fresh food at another. If you have fish that normally swim and feed at different water levels, you will have to be sure to provide food to each of them. Surface-feeders will miss out if the only food you offer sinks quickly, and by the same token, the poor bottom-feeders will soon go hungry if everyone else snatches up all of the food before it reaches them. Don't assume that catfish, for instance, are able to survive only on scavenged food and algae. They must be fed fresh food of their own every day. Nocturnal fish who feed at night have to be given their own food, too. Some owners provide for them with a small additional feeding after the tank lights have been turned off and the daytime fish have dozed off.

PART FIVE

Keeping Your Fish Healthy

11

Maintaining a Healthy Environment

It's axiomatic that a healthy environment is essential to the maintenance of good health for any living creature. We have all become increasingly aware of the influence of the environment on our well-being. In order to live comfortably without putting dangerous stresses on our bodies, the air we breathe must be relatively clean and free from pollutants and other foreign materials; the temperature of our living quarters should be maintained at a level that's neither too hot nor too cold; we prefer not to live in excess, blazing light or in deep darkness; and last, but not least, we do not thrive if we are constantly startled and/or frightened by the sudden appearance of unknown or threatening noises or looming shapes in our vicinity. It's equally important to maintain a good, stress-free environment for the fish in our care. By preventing stress, you can avoid most of the disease problems of fish.

Outside the Tank

It's interesting that we often forget or overlook the importance of outside influences on our pets. Fish, in particular, are often perceived as being isolated and protected from the outside world—safe in their own little cocoonlike tanks.

For some reason, many people seem to think that fish can neither see or hear through glass. While they wouldn't think of suddenly plunging a frightening object into the tank itself, they do allow children, visitors, and even household cats to put their faces right up against the glass of the fish tank. They think nothing of placing a loud stereo speaker right above the aquarium, or repeatedly slamming a door right next to it. Or they regularly tap and bang on the glass sides to "make the fish move."

Although most fish cannot see clear detail beyond about two feet, they certainly are able to detect objects and movement from a distance. Because they have no eyelids, movement and changes in light are visible even when fish are at rest. Rapid movements and large shapes that appear suddenly right outside the tank are certain to startle most fish and can seriously alarm the more skittish, shy individuals.

Sudden loud noises can have an even more frightening effect. Vibrations and sounds travel through water much more quickly than they do through air and are greatly magnified. (Remember the childrens' game of hitting small rocks together underwater, and what a loud noise it made?) As mentioned repeatedly, stress in any form will diminish a fish's ability to withstand illness and infection. A seriously startled fish may even do itself physical damage by banging against objects in the tank or even the glass itself in an effort to get away.

This doesn't mean that you have to maintain a deadly

silence in your fish room, or never allow anyone to approach the tank too closely. But it is best to go slow, especially when your fish are new to the tank or the tank is in a new location. Soon you'll learn how to avoid startling your fish, and as they become more comfortable in their new environment, they'll gradually learn to accept a certain level of disturbance. If you're lucky, your fish will begin to recognize you and other family members as you approach the tank and will even come to the side or top of the tank to greet you.

But if your fish continue to be extremely skittish and fearful, perhaps the tank should be relocated into a less traveled, less noisy area. Most fish will fare better in a relatively quiet living room, for example, than in the family room where children congregate and the TV or stereo play long and loud.

AIR POLLUTION?

Dr. Stoskopf says, "Smoking is very bad for fish." So is using glass cleaners with ammonia in them on the outside surface of the tank, spraying flea killer on your cat or dog in the same room, applying paint remover to a nearby bookshelf, using aerosol air fresheners or furniture polish, or gluing a toy plane with model cement on an adjacent desk. All of these fumes can be toxic to fish.

Fish can be made very seriously ill from air pollution or from toxic chemical fumes near the tank or in the surrounding room. How can that be, when the fish are swimming around in their climate-controlled, clean, filtered water? There are two ways in which airborne toxins can get into the water of an aquarium. First, they can enter through the surface of the water itself. Even if there is a fairly tight-fitting cover on the tank, fumes from strong cleansers, bug bombs, paint, or smoke from cigarettes, pipes, or cigars can easily seep in between the cracks. More serious, these toxins can be carried directly into the water via the very air pump and filter that are used to clean the water.

In the case of sudden toxicity, from insecticide or strong cleanser, for instance, all of the fish will quickly exhibit signs of illness. When the pollution is long-term, such as with continuous smoking or perhaps using an aerosol air freshener, the levels of toxin will build up gradually in the water. As the toxins accumulate, individual fish will mysteriously begin to sicken and gradually die. The first symptoms of trouble may not appear until up to a year of exposure has taken place.

Again, a common sense approach is called for. If Uncle Joe likes to smoke an after-dinner cigar, ask him to do so in another room. And, if it's necessary to use a chemical or paint spray in the same room with the aquarium, open the window and cover the tank tightly with plastic, leaving a pocket of air at the top. Leave the plastic in place until the fumes clear, but not for too long, however, because the fresh air inside the pocket will soon be exhausted.

Amount of Light

We talk about amounts of light in *Chapter Four*, and mentioned that a gradual light change will avoid stressing your fish. But, after you have your aquarium set up and running and the fish are in residence, you may have to readjust the lighting. If you find that there is an excessive growth of algae, for instance, you will need to cut back on either the degree of light you are using, or on the number of hours that you illuminate the tank. After cleaning off the algae, reduce the lighting a bit and see how fast the algae grows back. You may have to reduce the lighting several times until you've reached the ideal level and amount.

You will also need to reduce the light in your aquarium if your fish seem to be constantly restless and nervous. It may be that you have not provided sufficient hiding places or shade for those individuals that need lower light levels.

There are no hard and fast rules about the amount of light that a given aquarium should have. Based on careful observation, you are the only one who can adjust the light properly for your particular setup. Once you have achieved a desirable level of lighting, be sure to keep the bulbs clean and the reflector dry, clean, and free of dust, and protect the light from splashing water with a cover glass. The glass, too, needs to be cleaned of splashes and algae regularly so that the light can get through it. Replace any bulbs that have become dim.

The Right Temperature

No matter how good your water heater may be, the water temperature should be checked daily because mechanical failures can occur. In addition, sudden changes in the temperature of the surrounding room can put a big strain on your equipment. In very hot weather, you may have to protect your aquarium by completely shading it from the sun's rays which will heat it up too much. In excessive cold, you may need to insulate the tank, as described in *Chapter Four*.

Rapid temperature changes are extremely stressful for fish and may cause sudden death. If the temperature change is gradual, as it will be in a large tank, it is usually not immediately fatal, but can cause long-term damage to the fish. Too-cold water will make fish sluggish, anorexic, and highly susceptible to disease. When water is too warm the amount of dissolved oxygen in it will be decreased and, without extra aeration, a great strain will be put on the fish, which cannot breathe properly and will soon be gasping for air. In the long run, too-warm water will cause your fish to age faster. (Very warm water can, however, be useful in treating certain diseases and parasitic conditions, which will be discussed in *Chapter Twelve*.)

Filters and Pumps

The air pump and filter are the lifelines of your fish and only if they are working properly can they keep the water clean and well-aerated. No matter what type of equipment you have, it will require some regular maintenance in order to continue to function well. How often you need to do this depends in part on the size of the aquarium and the number of fish that you have in it.

Before doing any work at all on a pump, be sure to unplug it. Some pumps require regular cleaning and lubricating, while others are permanently sealed. Follow the manufacturer's instructions as to lubrication and cleaning. While cleaning the pump, check the valves and tubes and scrape out any algae or other matter that may have accumulated in them.

Box-type filters will need the filtering agent—floss or foam—cleaned or changed frequently, depending on the amount of dirt they have collected. The activated carbon must also be replaced from time to time, again, according to the amount of fish and general cleanliness of your aquarium.

Biological filters should not be cleaned more often than necessary, but the gravel over them should be raked regularly to loosen excess detritus which can then be removed with a siphon. If a biological filter should have to be cleaned, rinse it with cold water in order to kill as little of the useful bacteria as possible.

Other Maintenance Tasks

No matter whether or not you have an undergravel filtering system, the gravel in your aquarium should be cleaned—raked and siphoned, or vacuumed with a special gravel cleaner—regularly, once a week if you have a lot of fish and waste, less often if you have a sparsely occupied tank. You can easily check to see if the gravel needs cleaning by stirring up a small area. Don't put off this task, because excess decaying wastes will soon pollute the water.

Check to be sure that all of your fish are still swimming around. It can be very easy to overlook the absence of one small fish, but if that fish has died, it must be removed from the tank immediately before it begins to decay and to infect the remaining fish with whatever disease it died of. While you're at it, look each fish over carefully for any signs that all is not well. If any one looks ill, remove it to your hospital tank for observation and/or possible treatment before it infects its tank mates.

If you have live plants in your aquarium, look them over at least once a week. Remove any dead parts, trim any plants that are becoming overgrown, and remove excess algae from the leaves with a clean, soft brush that you reserve for this purpose.

If there is an excessive amount of algae on the front glass, you will have to remove it with a scraper. Although some algae is useful as food for certain fish, too much of it robs the water of oxygen. If the tank furnishings are overly "algaed,'' you can take them out and wash them in a solution of household bleach and water. (Remember, don't use soap!) Be sure to rinse them thoroughly several times in clear water to remove the bleach—porous objects should be soaked in clear water for several days before putting them back in the tank. Although there are algicides on the market, they should be used with caution because they may alter the water chemistry. It's far better to control excessive algae growth by cutting back on the light. Blue-green, fishy-smelling algae sometimes grow on the gravel at the bottom of aquariums. This is due to a lack of oxygen, caused by overfertilization because of excess waste, coupled with a lack of water motion. Fish do not eat this kind of algae, and they will kill any plants that they attack. They must be siphoned completely off and all of the waste removed or they will grow right back. If this kind of algae growth persists, you may need a stronger filtration system in addition to better cleaning habits.

Water Quality

Of course, the most important environmental influence on your fish is the water that they live in and it must be maintained at the best level possible. To ensure that its chemistry is correct, you need to test the water regularly. When you first start up your aquarium, it's best to test the pH and nitrite levels on a weekly basis and after every time that you make a partial water change. You may also want to test for oxygen and carbon dioxide levels at the same time. Once your aquarium has been up and running for a while, you can probably safely cut down on the frequency of testing, although you should still test the water after every change. Of course, if there is a problem with the water chemistry, you should correct it right away and continue to test the water on a daily basis until it reaches the correct levels. In addition to products that will change the hardness and pH of the water, there are water conditioners that will remove toxins, and special ammonia absorbers (usually consisting of zeolite) that are very useful when used with a biological filter in reducing the number of water changes needed.

WATER PROBLEMS

Discolored water of any sort indicates some kind of problem or imbalance in the aquarium.

If the water in your tank suddenly turns very cloudy, it is probably because of a bacterial buildup, or "bloom," caused by too many nutrients in the water. Overfeeding of dry food, overcrowding, and excess plant wastes can all contribute to this problem. Sometimes this occurs when there is not enough gravel covering an undergravel filtration system and/or the filter has not been in place long enough to become properly seasoned. Cloudy water can also be the result of organic contamination from improperly rinsed gravel, or unclean tank decorations.

Green water is caused by an algae "bloom." Again, this may be attributed to large amounts of decaying organic matter, but is usually the result of too much light.

WATER CHANGES

The best way to maintain good water quality is to make partial water changes on a regular basis. Not only will this replace water that will be naturally lost through evaporation, but it will replace the old, stagnant water with fresh and remove or dilute dissolved wastes in the process.

There are no firm rules as to how much water to change,

nor how often to change it. A great deal depends on the size of your tank, the number of fish in it, how heavily they eat, the amount of their waste, and so forth. For example, large, messy fish like cichlids will need more of their water changed much more frequently than the average community tank of small fish. A 20-gallon tank with one big oscar in it can need a 50 percent change of water three times a week, for instance. The general rule of thumb is to change about 20 to 30 percent of the water in the average 20-gallon community aquarium every three-to-four weeks, but the only way to make an intelligent decision about *your* particular setup is to test the water regularly and change it when needed. Soon, you'll be able to develop a regular schedule. Because changing the water can be so beneficial for fish, it is often recommended that 50 percent or more of the water be changed if there is a serious problem in an aquarium.

When changing water, always take the old water out of the bottom of the tank with a siphon in order to remove the most wastes. There are several kinds of water-changing equipment on the market that remove old water from the bottom of the tank while simultaneously adding fresh water at the surface, but most people simply use a siphon and bucket. After a sufficient amount of dirty water has been removed by siphon from the bottom, fresh water that has already been prepared (chlorine or chloramine removed, proper water chemistry and temperature established) is poured on top gradually. Avoid pouring the water in too quickly or it will disturb the substrate, plantings, and furnishings, to say nothing of the fish themselves. Some people advocate using untreated room-temperature tap water as a replacement, but in a small tank this could upset the water chemistry and temperature enough to seriously hurt the fish.

Summary of Maintenance Tasks

On a Daily Basis:

>   Check the temperature of the water.
>   Remove all uneaten food with a siphon.
>   Check the tank visually for dead or diseased fish—
>   remove immediately.
>   Check to be sure that all equipment is running properly.

On a Weekly Basis:

>   Clean filter-box material if needed.
>   Rake gravel and remove detritus with a siphon.
>   Clean cover glass.
>   Check light fixture and bulbs—clean or replace if needed.
>   Test water chemistry; adjust if necessary.
>   Remove dead parts from plants; trim if needed.
>   Remove excess algae.

On a Regular Basis—as Needed

>   Clean and lubricate pump.
>   Do a partial water change.

Keeping a Record

Although maintaining a fish tank is not difficult, at first
there may seem to be a lot of different steps involved until
you get the hang of it. It's a good idea to establish a notebook or folder in which you can check off the various tasks
each time that you do them. This can be especially helpful

for youngsters who are learning to take care of an aquarium on their own.

There's another good reason for keeping careful notes about water chemistry, water changes, and any water treatments that you may have performed: these notes can be very useful in the future if you start up another aquarium or want to help a friend to begin the hobby.

Of course, if you have to give any medications, a permanent record for future reference will be invaluable, and the same holds true if you decide that you want to get into breeding your fish.

12

Diseases and Disorders of Fish

Just as all other animals do, fish get sick. And, just as with other pets, the only way that you will be able to tell if your fish are not well is if you know how they look and act normally. If you have observed your fish as they eat, after they eat (when their breathing rate may increase), as they interact with each other, and when they are swimming around in the aquarium during different times of the day, you will be better able to spot any change in their normal activities and behavior quickly. It is a very good idea to keep notes about your fish and their everyday behavior along with those that you make about water treatment. Because many fish diseases are highly contagious, early detection of trouble can make a big difference, not only to save the life of one individual, but to save the entire population of your aquarium. The best route, however, is to prevent illness and infection from occurring at all.

Preventing Illness

Because environmental stress lowers a fish's resistance to disease, all of the things that have been talked about in the previous chapters can help to keep the fish in your tank from getting sick. Contamination from outside of the tank can also cause trouble—dirty hands, equipment, and disease-carriers in the form of live food and new fish can all introduce parasites and disease organisms into your aquarium. As a reminder, here's a checklist of important illness-preventing rules:

- Keep the tank clean—free from wastes and other pollutants. No overfeeding.
- Don't overcrowd the aquarium.
- Perform adequate water changes when needed.
- Don't introduce parasites and disease organisms to your aquarium. Wash/sterilize equipment, nets, plants, furnishings. Feed only clean live food.
- Use a quarantine tank when introducing new fish.
- Keep the water temperature consistently warm enough— allow no big fluctuations in temperature. Avoid chilling.
- Immediately remove any fish that exhibits signs of infection or illness from the main tank and place in a hospital tank.

Signs of Illness

Dr. Stoskopf notes, "If the first sign of illness that you notice is your fish floating upside-down, it won't do you much good—that's pretty tough to fix." He tells one story about floating fish, however, that does have a happy ending.

Late one night, he had a frantic telephone call from a fish-owning friend who was in the midst of a move from Denver to the western part of Colorado. The friend had carefully packed his fish for the trip (see *Chapter Sixteen*). When he reached the top of a high mountain pass, he stopped the car and decided to check his fish. To his horror, when he opened the container, all of his fish were floating at the surface of the water! That's when he called Dr. Stoskopf in a panic. After finding out just where he was calling from, it didn't take long to figure out what the problem was, and the fish owner was reassured that once he drove back down the other side of the pass the fish would be all right. Dr. Stoskopf explained that, as the car had ascended quickly to higher and higher altitudes, the change in air pressure had caused the fish's swim-bladders to expand—they couldn't adapt fast enough to the rapid lowering of pressure and therefore floated right up to the water's surface. Once they were back down at ground level, they were fine—their swim-bladders adjusted, and they were able to swim at their normal water levels again. Most of the time, though, when a fish is floating on the water's surface, it's too late to help it.

The only way that you'll avoid this extreme is to learn to recognize when all is not right with your fish. Some signs are pretty obvious, but others are more subtle.

Often, the first symptoms of illness that you'll observe are changes in behavior, attitude, or posture in one or more of your fish.

Some of the first symptoms of illness are:

Anorexia, or loss of appetite—This may be difficult to recognize right away unless you regularly observe your fish as they eat. Loss of appetite in a formerly healthy eater is a serious sign of a number of systemic illnesses and disorders, and, often, it is too late to do much by the time it is noticed.

Breathing difficulty, rapid gill movements, gasping, air-gulping at the surface—These actions may signify gill disease or parasite infestation, poisoning, poor water quality such as lack of sufficient oxygen, or many systemic infections and diseases.

Fins held close to the body rather than erect—This is a sure sign that a fish is either not happy or not well. A fish that is constantly being picked on may clamp its fins against its body in order to avoid further attacks, but fin-clamping is also often a symptom of illness.

Loss of Equilibrium or buoyancy (bottom-sitting, head-standing, leaning over in the water, swimming at a different level than usual)—all of these behaviors can be caused by a number of different abdominal and swim-bladder problems, such as a gas accumulation due to a severe bacterial or parasitic infection or tuberculosis. Lateral-line problems can cause leaning and other abnormal swimming positions.

Loss of strength, drifting, lethargy, and bottom-sitting can signify poisoning and serious illness. (Be sure that the fish is not simply sleeping or resting.)

Restlessness, jerkiness, sudden spurts of swimming and strange/odd swimming behavior—all signs of severe poisoning or serious disease. "Shimmying" is usually due to improper water conditions (water too cold and too soft), and is often seen in mollies.

Rubbing against objects and/or the tank bottom—means a fish is suffering from an itchy parasitic infestation, such as flukes or worms.

Physical indications that all is not well are:

Color change—This can be behavioral if it occurs during courtship and spawning activity. Otherwise, color loss indicates that a fish is feeling poorly, either due to a lack of oxygen in the water or a systemic illness. Sudden darkening can signal infection, and white patches along a marine fish's sides are signs of lateral-line disease.

Eyes cloudy—Parasitic or bacterial disease.

Eyes popping—Systemic disease, such as septicemia or tuberculosis, or a tumor.

Fins ragged—This can be due to fin-nipping by other fish, or may be a sign of tuberculosis, fin rot, or lateral-line disease in marine fish.

Gills thickened, flared, or swollen—This is caused by irritation due to infection or a parasite infestation.

Lumps, bumps, growths—Usually tumors, but may be caused by worms or a bacterial disease.

Slime, dots, white tufts on the skin—All signs of various bacterial, parasitic, or fungal diseases.

Swelling, distention of the abdomen—Can be due to "dropsy," or ascites, and internal tumors.

Wasting, or hollow-looking abdomen—Can be due to a poor or insufficient diet, but is usually caused by a systemic disease, internal tumor, or severe internal worm infestation.

Tank-Wide Problems

If all of the fish in your tank suddenly start to look strange or to behave oddly, you should immediately suspect some kind of serious problem with the water in the aquarium. If the problem is severe and sudden, all of the fish will exhibit signs of difficulty at once. If it is chronic, you will probably notice that the more delicate individuals succumb first, eventually followed by the entire population.

The most common problem in a freshwater aquarium is some kind of *poisoning* of the water. Airborne pollutants, dissolved metals in the water from pipes of equipment that's in contact with the water, unclean or inappropriate tank furnishings or decorations can all cause fish to become ill. In addition to sudden death, there are a number of signs of poisoning in fish—they may swim in an erratic way, chasing and dashing about, gasp for air, or lose their appetites, among other things. You may be able to save the fish if you act quickly to remove the problem and perform a water change.

Ammonia intoxication or nitrite poisoning are very common occurrences when there is overcrowding, overfeeding, lack of proper cleaning and/or inadequate filtration. Affected fish will lose their appetites, breathe with difficulty, gasp, chase and dash around wildly, even swim upside-down and whirling about. They may also darken in color. If detected in time, the fish may be able to be saved by adjusting the water quality quickly with appropriate treatments and partial changes. If the pH level of the water is too high or too low, it can also cause fish to exhibit signs of poisoning and will eventually damage their gills. Affected fish may try to jump out of the water, as they also will if the oxygen levels become too low.

If the temperature in your aquarium is too low, all of the fish will appear lethargic and will loose their appetites.

Kinds of Illnesses and Diseases

There are far too many diseases of fish to begin to mention them all in this book, but some of the more common are:

PARASITIC DISEASES

By far the largest category of disease to which ornamental fish are prey is parasitic diseases. Most fish parasites are what are called "opportunistic," that is, they will attack an animal that has already been weakened in one way or another—by poor living conditions, a wound or injury, or other systemic, bacterial, or viral disease.
Often-seen parasitic diseases of fish are:

Protozoan Parasites—All of these parasites are highly contagious:

Costia is one of several parasites that are referred to as "slime disease," because infected individuals produce excess mucus that causes a grayish slime on their bodies. Fish may also suffer from weakness and breathing problems.

Ich, or **White Spot Disease,** is probably the most commonly seen disease of freshwater aquarium fish. Saltwater fish are also afflicted with white spot, although the causative parasite is different. In both cases, the fish's skin is covered with tiny white spots. Badly affected individuals will also develop breathing difficulties.

Velvet Disease, Gold-dust Disease, Rust Disease, are all caused by a species of parasites called Oodinium, one of which also causes **Coral Fish Disease** in marine fish. Fish with this disease have gills and skin covered with a fine, gold- or rust-colored dusty

167

powder. The gills may move rapidly. The disease can be treated with appropriate medication.

Other External Parasites:

Hole-in-the-Head Disease is often seen in association with the intestinal parasite Hexamita, but the parasite is not thought to be the primary cause of the disease, which is associated with poor tank conditions and an inadequate diet. Cichlids are most often affected. The disease attacks the internal organs and symptoms include anorexia, loss of weight, and lesions on the head and face. The parasite can be eradicated, but if internal damage has been done it may be too late to save an individual fish. Proper tank care can prevent this disease.

Neon Tetra Disease causes fish to lose color, become very emaciated, and die. It is caused by a tiny parasite called Plistophora, and affects all characins and sometimes angelfish, barbs, danios, and rasboras, as well as tetras. It is highly contagious and usually fatal.

External Parasitic Worms and Crustaceans:

Anchor Worms are tiny crustaceans that bury their heads in the flesh of the fish, leaving threadlike egg sacs dangling outside. The fish will try to scrape the worms off, and the area around the worm may become irritated. Koi and goldfish are particularly susceptible to anchor worm infestation. The worms must be removed with a tweezer and the affected area of skin disinfected.

Fish Lice are also crustaceans that attach themselves to fish with suckers through which they sting the fish's skin. Symptoms and treatment are similar to those for anchor worms.

Flukes, gill or skin, are caused by related parasitic worms that burrow into the skin or gills, causing extreme irritation and an increased production of mucus. Affected fish will be itchy and try to rid themselves of the worms. Those with gill flukes will display swollen gills and wide-open gill covers.

Internal Parasites:

Intestinal Worms such as roundworms and tapeworms do attack fish. They are usually introduced into an aquarium in live food. The only external sign of a worm infestation is if the worms are seen sticking out of a fish's anus. Badly infected fish will be anemic, lose their appetites, and become emaciated. Worms can be difficult to treat, but may respond to appropriate medication.

FUNGAL DISEASES

Fungi are plants that grow on organic matter, and fish are usually invaded by fungal disease when they have suffered from an injury—a sore caused by a parasite, for example. Fish affected with fungal growth will be covered with cottony tufts of white material or a film of grayish-looking matter. The fungi can be killed, but the reason for the attack must be determined and eradicated, or the fungus will return.

BACTERIAL DISEASES

Bacterial infections can affect a fish internally or externally and are often the result of stress, poor water, and diet. In general, external bacterial infections are secondary to parasitic infestations. They may be able to be helped with antibiotic treatment. Internal bacterial diseases are very difficult to treat, especially in freshwater fish (see *Medicating Fish, page 176*), and usually have progressed too far for successful treatment before they are detected.

Commonly seen external bacterial diseases are:

Fin Rot tends to affect species with long, flowing fins and tails and dark pigmentation. The infection can arise when fins are damaged by nipping, but is usually attributable to poor water conditions. The skin is destroyed, and fins and tail appear frayed. Appropriate medications may help, but the underlying cause must be corrected or the condition will reappear.

Mouth "Fungus," or **Cotton Mouth Disease**, is not a fungus, but a bacterial infection that primarily affects livebearers kept in improper water conditions. The slime bacteria form white threads that appear round and above the fish's mouth.

Internal bacterial diseases:

Dropsy is a condition in which a fish's abdomen becomes distended, causing the scales to stick out all over the body. It is often impossible to determine the exact cause of this condition. It may be due to septicemia, a condition in which tissue is destroyed due to disease-causing bacteria (loosely described as "blood poisoning"), which is usually a secondary infection following fin rot or another bacterial infection. Sometimes, a viral infection is also involved. Depending on the cause, it may or may not be contagious. Isolation and veterinary help is recommended, but by the time that symptoms appear it is usually too late to save a fish. Affected fish should be removed from the tank and the tank treated to avoid spread of the infection.

Tuberculosis is an infectious bacterial disease that is very common in aquarium fish. Some signs of the disease are weight loss while feeding normally, dull color, deformities of the skeleton, and skin lesions and popped eyes due to subcutaneous nodules. Many fish carry latent nodules of the disease that only surface when aquarium conditions deteriorate. The disease is incurable, and affected fish should be immediately removed from the tank before they infect the other inhabitants. If a fish is suspected of dying from the disease, a postmortem diagnosis should be made, and all exposed fish should be removed from the tank and treated or destroyed, and the aquarium disinfected before introducing any new fish.

VIRAL DISEASES

There is very little known about viral diseases of fish, but one disease, **Lymphocystis,** has been isolated. This disease affects saltwater fish more often than those that live in freshwater, and causes tumorlike nodules to grow on fins and tail. Local applications of appropriate medication may help to control the disease, and affected fins will grow back.

There is also a common, chronic radioviral disease called **Spring Viraemia of Carp (SVC)** that affects goldfish and koi when their immune system is low and can cause them to be more susceptible to other infections. There is no cure. Affected fish's scales stick up all over their bodies.

mor that can sometimes be treated with success is a thyroid gland tumor. In general, however, fish with tumors must be destroyed.

Making a Diagnosis

Of course, you cannot hope to help your fish to get better if you don't know why they're sick or what, exactly, they may be suffering from. Needless to say, if the problem is bacterial, an antifungal medication will do no good at all and will simply waste valuable time—more about medications later in this chapter.

It may help you to assess the problem if you sit down and write out an analysis of your aquarium. Unless only one or two fish are involved, Dr. Stoskopf recommends making up a *tank record*, such as the one in *Table 2*. The significance of a lot of the information in *Table 2* is fairly clear. If a tank is new, small, and overloaded, for instance, the trouble is quite obvious. And, if you're using a biological filter and it's only been in operation for a short while, it probably hasn't reached peak efficiency yet. The temperature of the water must be correct for the kind of fish that you're keeping. Some owners scrimp on heating as an economy measure—they should realize that, if the water is consistently kept too cold, the fish are going to be constantly run down and susceptible to disease. In an article called "Taking the History"[1] (directed toward veterinarians, the information can be useful for fish owners as well), Dr. Stoskopf points out that "sedimentary rocks, inappropriate gravel,

---

1. Michael K. Stoskopf, DVM, PhD, "Taking the History," *The Veterinary Clinics of North America, Small Animal Practice*, Volume 18/Number 2, March 1988. Tropical Fish Medicine, Michael K. Stoskopf, DVM, PhD, Guest Editor. Philadelphia: W. B. Saunders Company.

Table 2— **Basic Questions To Ask Yourself When Your Fish Are Ill—A Tank Record**

About the Tank
How big is it?
How long has it been set up?
Does it have a top? Where is it?
What type of gravel does it have?
What type of filters does it have?
What type of heater does it have?
What temperature is the tank kept at?
Are there any decorations in the tank? What are they?

About the Water
How often do you change the water?
How much do you change? How do you do it?
What water do you use when you make changes?
What type of water pipes do you have in your house? Copper? Galvanized? Lead?
What water tests do you do? What are your current values for these tests?

About the Fish
What fish are in the tank?
Have any died recently? How many? Which ones?
Are they eating well?
What do you feed them? How often?
What are the fish doing?
Are all of the fish affected?
Do you see any spots, tufts?
Are the fins ragged?
How do the fish swim?
Do they appear depressed?
Where do they stay in the tank?

Epidemiologic Questions
Have you added any new fish recently? When?
How are these new fish?
Are there any plants in the tank? Any new ones?
Are there snails in the tank?
Have there been any other changes in the tank or in the area surrounding it?

Adapted from: Michael K. Stoskopf, DVM, PhD, "Taking the History," *The Veterinary Clinics of North America, Small Animal Practice*, Volume 18/Number 2, March 1988, p. 289. Tropical Fish Medicine, Michael K. Stoskopf, DVM, PhD, Guest Editor. Philadelphia; W. B. Saunders Company.

173

and unusual or painted decorations can introduce toxic levels of heavy metals and other poisons.''

In regard to a top on the tank, he goes on to say, "In a new tank, a very meticulously fitted top (or cover glass), combined with a tank filled to the brim may be limiting air exchange . . . Likewise, an older tank may be collecting anything from peeling paint chips to carpet lint with fire retardant if it doesn't have a top.''

Thinking about the air pump will serve to remind you that the air that it's sending into the water is gathered from the room and that any toxins that may be in the room air will be sent into the water. When there is "accumulated toxin" in the water, the fish will gradually die after a fairly long period.

Accumulated toxins can also be internal, and improper water changes are the culprit. In the case of mysterious deaths over a period of time, you may have to ask yourself some detailed questions about the water that you are adding to your aquarium. It's highly possible that your water pipes are leaching heavy metals into the water that are slowly poisoning your fish tank.

The mixture of fish in your aquarium may also be a cause of difficulty. If you have insisted on housing fish that require very different water conditions in the same tank, you may have set the stage for health problems. If some fish are required to live in less-than-ideal conditions they will soon become stressed and susceptible to illness.

Of course, "The presence of intermediate hosts (snails and tubifex worms, for example) and/or other infectious disease vectors (plants and new fish)" should immediately be suspected as causes of disease.

Dr. Stoskopf points out that there are many more diseases of fish than symptoms, so that diagnosis can be very difficult. Often, the best the average fish keeper can do is to identify the *kind* of disease that an individual fish or an entire population of fish are suffering from. A frustrating situation that occurs frequently is when you seem to have cured a fish of a disease, or to have finally gotten your tank back to rights, only to have the problem resurface a month or two later. At this point you must make a decision. If you have a valuable collection or an individual fish about which you care a great deal you may want to take the time and possible expense of seeking outside help.

GETTING HELP

There are various avenues that you can take to help you to identify a problem. If it's a tank-wide one that you can't figure out, take a sample of the water, or, if a fish has died, put it into a plastic bag with ice. Call your fish dealer and ask if he'll help. It's possible that his experience and equipment may enable him to find out more about the water chemistry than you can and help you to adjust the water correctly, and he'll be able to identify the majority of illnesses that have killed your fish.

If you're lucky enough to have a public aquarium nearby, it is usually part of their educational mission to help individual fish keepers out of difficulty. They can be especially helpful if you have an ongoing problem. Don't hesitate to call them and be prepared to give them a thorough history— *Table 2* (see *page 173*) can help you to include all of the relevant data. If they're close enough, you may want to take a water sample and/or fish to them.

Aquarium societies can also be of help. If you've already joined one, call and ask for any information that they might have that's relevant to your problem. They may be able to put you in touch with individuals who've had the same, or similar, problems.

MORE SOPHISTICATED HELP

Until recently, there was little that the average fish keeper could actually do to treat a fish once it came down with an illness—except to remove it from the aquarium, treat the water, and hope that the rest of the fish in the tank didn't get sick too. As the hobby of fish keeping has grown and people are breeding and buying valuable specimens of fish—a large koi may sell for ten to twenty thousand dollars, for instance—there are an increasing number of avenues of help available when a fish is ailing. What's more, the proliferation of commercial breeders/farmers of ornamental fish has added to the demand for professional health care. More research into the diagnosis, treatment, and prevention of fish disease is currently being performed.

Although the number of veterinarians who actually treat fish is small, it is growing. According to Dr. Stoskopf, "More than half of the veterinary schools [in the United States] are now providing training for some of their students in fish medicine." If you already have a veterinarian for other pets, call him. Even if he doesn't treat fish himself, he may know someone who does. There are now some quite sophisticated computer programs available to veterinarians to help them diagnose fish illnesses.

There is also a software program that individuals with modems can subscribe to called *Fishnet*. Many people who are really involved in the hobby of fish keeping use this program to exchange valuable information about all kinds of problems and concerns, including illness. (See *Appendix B* for more information.)

Medicating Fish

It's clear that the first thing to do is to look at the environment when more than one or two fish are ill *before* you attempt to medicate the fish. The very first thing that you should do if trouble appears is to test the water. Often, if you simply make sure that the water is warm enough and perform one or more partial water changes the problem will be solved. Dr. Stoskopf points out that one of the reasons commercial treatments seem to work is that they usually contain instructions such as, "Be sure that the temperature of the tank remains steady," and, "Change half of the water every day." These steps alone may very well make the fish better.

You should bear some things in mind before you start to dump medicines into your fish tank. Too much medication in the water can harm, rather than help, the fish. Many chemicals can damage fish's gills, for instance. You should also know that most medications will kill live plants; copper-based medicines will kill saltwater invertebrates; antibiotics will destroy the good bacteria in a biological filter along with the bad ones, and, as Daniel Bebak reminds: if you are going to medicate the water in an aquarium, remove activated carbon from your filter because the carbon will remove the medicine from the water.

If the problem is not tank-wide, but is limited to only one or several individuals, remove the affected fish from the main aquarium and put them into a hospital tank for treatment. In order not to damage the scales or mucus covering of an already stressed fish, many people recommend using a plastic bag to capture the fish, rather than a net. Because so many diseases are stress-related or stress-induced, the hospital tank should be placed in a very quiet room. Alternatively, you can cover the outside of the tank with some opaque material so that the fish cannot see any activity going on around the aquarium. Unless you know for sure that all the fish have a contagious illness, there's no need to treat the entire main tank, and unnecessary medication will upset the tank's biological balance. However, it is good practice to change the water partially, just to be on the safe side. Of course, if you know that a disease is contagious or infectious, you'll have to give the main tank prophylactic treatment to avoid the spread of the disease.

Over-the-counter medications that are sold in fish stores vary tremendously in efficacy. The real problem is that there is no government regulation of these medicines and many of them have been on the shelf too long. Many are sold in prepared mixtures that may not be in the right proportions or strengths for your particular problem.

However, most fish medicines that are sold for the treatment of parasites work pretty well. They are usually dissolved in the tank water and will act to interrupt the life cycle of the parasite by destroying one or more of its life stages. Many experts recommend formalin baths for fish affected with various parasitic infestations, or freshwater baths for saltwater fish and saltwater baths for freshwater individuals. (See *page 179* for a definition of a "bath.") External parasites such as anchor worms must be removed from the fish. The fish will have to be picked up out of the water so that this can be done. Often, the fish is anesthetized by injection or in a bath—a job for a veterinarian or very experienced fish keeper to perform.

In general, commercially sold antibiotics are not effective. In addition to the possibility that they are outdated, they are usually sold in concentrations that are so low that they can do no good. If you find yourself in a situation where you know that you need antibiotics for your fish, go to your veterinarian (or, if you don't have a veterinarian, your own physician) and explain the problem. He will probably be able to give you an appropriate prescription.

Appropriate broad-based antibiotics work well on external bacterial infections. A problem arises if you want to get antibiotics inside a freshwater fish for a systemic infection. Dosing the food is not usually effective—the fish may be off its food to begin with, and it is very difficult to be sure that it eats the right amount of food in any case. Because of osmosis, freshwater fish drink very little water, so dosing the aquarium water won't get any medicine into them. Dr. Loiselle says that there are some new antibiotics on the market with a sufficiently small molecular structure so that they can be absorbed by a fish's gills. The most commonly available of these is minicycline hydrachloride and he suggests asking your veterinarian or physician about this if you need an antibiotic treatment for your fish. No matter how good the antibiotic may be, it won't do any good unless you can get it into the fish. Saltwater fish, on the other hand, do drink water and can, therefore, be helped by antibiotics in solution.

Ways to Medicate Fish

There are several ways of medicating fish:

Entire Tank Treatment—This is the most often-used type of treatment, in which a drug is put directly in solution in the water. Although this is a simple method, these remedies often contain dyes, and can lead to a big clean-up job, and may kill plants and spoil biological filtration. Because the solution is usually quite weak, it is also usually not particularly effective.

Baths and Dips—A separate tank or other container is

necessary in order to perform a bath or dip. A very short dip in and out of medication works only to destroy a localized parasite of some kind. A bath can be long or short, according to the problem. The fish is removed from the main tank and placed in the bath for a certain period of time—anywhere from five minutes to an hour. Because the medication in a bath is designed to kill parasites, it is quite strong, so the fish should be watched all of the time that it's in the solution. If the fish shows ill effects it can be removed from the bath and put back into the main tank right away. The medication used can be of whatever strength is deemed necessary, and the main aquarium does not need to be treated.

Treating a Fish Out of the Water—A fish can be taken out of the water in a net, plastic bag, or wet cloth so that medication can be applied directly to an affected spot. A wound, for instance, or severe fin rot, can be treated this way. Care must be taken not to damage the scales, and the fish should be returned to a hospital tank to recuperate.

In the case of wounds that might need longer treatment, or if a tumor or other growth needs to be removed, fish can be *anesthetized*. There are two ways to do this, by putting the anesthetic in the water with the fish, or by injecting the fish with the anesthetic. Fish can also be given medication by *injection*, although only by experienced veterinarians or fish handlers.

Medications can be administered *in food*, but it is, of course, necessary for the fish to still be eating well in order to do this. There are commercial fish foods that have medications in them. Problems can arise if the fish do not like the food, won't eat it at all, and starve themselves, so careful observation is essential if you are going to use this method.

One further method of treating fish must be mentioned here. On January 14, 1989, Ashley Dunn reported in the *Los Angeles Times* that two Chinese acupuncturists, Cho Sheng-gung and Wu Li-hsia, have been experimenting with acupuncture to cure ailing goldfish. The treatment was given to 12 fish in an aquarium in which one had already died. The 12 fish recovered, much to the surprise of everyone, including the acupuncturists themselves!

Can You Catch a Disease From Your Fish?

Most fish diseases are what are called "species-specific," that is, they are not able to be transmitted to other species. The fact remains, however, that there are always exceptions, and cleanliness is important when handling any animal, especially if it is not well. It's a good basic rule to always wash your hands before and after handling fish, equipment, and filter material. If you have an open wound on your hands, it's a good idea to wear rubber gloves when working in an aquarium, and you should take care not to swallow any aquarium water when using a siphon tube.

In "Morbidity and Mortality Weekly Report," published by the Centers for Disease Control in Atlanta, Georgia, on September 15, 1989 (Vol. 38/No. 36), there is a story about a case in which a 14-month-old baby in Missouri contracted a mysterious bacterial infection that resulted in diarrhea and fever. After investigation, it evolved that she had been bathed in a bathtub into which her baby sitter regularly poured waste water from her aquarium when cleaning it. The bacteria that had caused the child's infection was isolated from the aquarium water. Based on this case, the Missouri Health Department issued a strong recommendation that tubs, sinks, or other containers into which water from an aquarium is regularly poured should be thoroughly scrubbed with chlorine bleach before they are used for any other purpose.

PART SIX

Other Kinds Of Fish

13

Coldwater Freshwater Fish

Many people like to keep freshwater fish that live in cold water, rather than a heated aquarium. There are several reasons why. For some, it's very appealing to be able to forgo the responsibility of having to maintain the correct temperatures for tropicals. Other people want to be able to keep their fish outdoors for at least some part of the year, and coldwater fish are the answer for everyone who doesn't live in a tropical climate. Still others keep coldwater fish simply because they like them.

There is not room in this book to explore the entire subject of coldwater fish keeping, but this chapter will contain a brief overview of the hobby.

Care of Coldwater Freshwater Fish

Most species of freshwater fish that live in cold, or unheated, water are omnivorous eaters. They are hardy, and quite tolerant of less-than-perfect water chemistry. They do, nevertheless, have certain requirements in order to thrive.

WATER

The chemical makeup of the water that they live in is not as important for coldwater fish as it is for tropicals. In general, they like water that is neither too hard nor too soft. Moderate hardness and a neutral range of pH, around 6.5 to 7.8, is best for them. If you live in an area where the water is either acid or alkaline, or very hard or soft, check with your fish dealer for advice. It is usually not essential to "season" the water for weeks before adding the fish to it (some varieties of fancy goldfish may be more delicate— follow your dealer's advice). However, it is still important not to overload any aquarium, container, or pond with a large number of fish all at once. Even a large outdoor pond must be given time to adjust to the ammonia load produced by fish—and many coldwater fish produce larger-than-average amounts of waste (see *The Nitrogen Cycle* in *Chapter Nine*).

If your tap water is treated with chlorine or chloramide, you will have to treat it to remove the chemicals before you add the fish to an indoor aquarium or small outdoor fish container (see *Chapter Six*). Allowing the water to sit for a few days with the plants in place will do the job in a bigger outdoor pond.

Partial water changes for aquariums and small outdoor containers are just as necessary in a cold water setup as they are in a tropical aquarium in order to remove wastes and refresh the water. Properly aged water should be added to replace anywhere from one-third to one-half of the water in a container or aquarium at least once a month. In a pond, adding fresh water to replace what's lost to evaporation will be sufficient.

SPACE

One of the biggest mistakes made with coldwater fish is overcrowding. These fish all require a lot of space in order to do well. Not only do they need more dissolved oxygen in the water to breathe comfortably, but they also eat a lot and therefore, give off a much larger amount of waste than tropicals do. On top of this, most freshwater species, especially goldfish and colored carp, or koi, grow very quickly so unless you conscientiously *understock*, your aquarium, container, or pond will soon become overcrowded. Under the right conditions, many species of goldfish can attain a size of ten inches, while koi may grow to be three feet in length.

A large surface is also needed for the proper exchange of gasses (see *Aquarium Size and Shape* in *Chapter Three*). The ubiquitous goldfish bowls, found in every five-and-ten and small pet shop, are an example of the very worst kind of container. The narrow, inward-slanting tops and small openings of these bowls not only provide a very small water surface, but also trap carbon dioxide and prevent it from escaping while at the same time impeding oxygen from entering the water. Sadly, goldfish kept in these kinds of bowls are continuously on the point of suffocating to death and are usually seen trying to suck in a little oxygen from the water's surface. It's rather amazing that any of them manage to survive at all—only the very hardiest do.

TEMPERATURE

Although you do not need to heat the water for coldwater fish, you do have to make sure that the temperature of the water doesn't get too high. For most species, a water temperature over 75° F. is too hot. As the water gets warmer, the level of dissolved oxygen in the water falls and increased aeration will be necessary for the fish to survive—coldwater fish require more oxygen than tropical fish do.

In outdoor ponds and containers, shade can help to keep the temperature of the water down in hot weather. If you place a pond directly under a tree, however, you'll continuously have to clean leaves and other debris from the surface. A filter (see *page 47*), aerator, or constant stream of fresh water through a waterfall, fountain, overflow, or other device will also help to cool and aerate the water.

One portion of a pond should be quite deep (two to three feet) so that the water at the bottom will remain cooler and provide a convenient place for the fish to go if it gets too warm. This will also prevent a solid freeze-up if you plan to "overwinter" your fish outdoors. In very warm climates it may be necessary to cool the water mechanically, especially in aquariums. There are mechanical coolers on the market designed for that purpose. A thermometer will ensure that you keep the water in the right temperature range.

Coldwater pond fish can safely stay outdoors in the winter in areas where it doesn't freeze. In colder climates, some people opt to bring their fish indoors in the winter—large specimens such as koi can be housed in a large wading pool or tub in a cool basement. If there are a lot of large fish, however, this can be quite a project, and many people leave their pond fish outdoors all year as long as there is an area that is deep enough so that it won't freeze all the way down. Many people then simply leave the pond alone until it thaws in spring. Others regularly break a hole in the ice to feed the fish and check up on them. In *Your Garden Pond*[1], Dr. Loiselle writes, "Even a thin layer of ice can inhibit gas

1. Weiser, K. H., and Loiselle, P. V., Dr., *Your Garden Pond, 1986.* Melle, West Germany and Morris Plains, NJ: Tetra-Press.

exchange [see *Chapter Three: Aquarium Size and Shape* for an explanation of this]. Two simple measures will go far toward eliminating this hazard.'' First, he recommends that you clean the pool bottom right after the first frost to remove any dead vegetation that would rob the water of oxygen as it decays, and siphon off any debris that remains. Second, if there are no tall reeds or grasses planted in your pond, put a weighted bundle of straw or reeds in the deep end of the pool so that they protrude above the top of the water. The stalks will keep the surface of the pond from freezing over completely and allow gas exchange to occur.

When the water is very cold, fish will become inactive and require little food.

FILTRATION

Filtration is absolutely necessary in an indoor aquarium containing freshwater fish. A power filter that uses activated carbon is usually best, because of the large amount of waste that these fish produce.

The question of filtration for an outdoor pond is widely discussed in fish-keeping circles. According to Dr. Loiselle, it is not necessary in a garden pond under ideal circumstances: that is, if the pond is large, and is not overstocked with fish that constantly stir up the plantings and/or the bottom. However, these ideal conditions may not exist and, in addition to fish loss, a pond-keeper may find that the water is so clouded and murky that he cannot even see the fish.

Dr. Loiselle recommends a pond filter in the following circumstances: if the water temperature regularly goes over 80° F. for more than a couple of days at a time; if the water temperature varies considerably in different parts of the pond; if there aren't enough plants to inhibit the growth of algae; if the fish constantly stir up the bottom; and if the pond contains a lot of fish, or a few very big fish.

There are filters on the market that are designed specifically for outdoor pond use. People who need special filtration for large ponds or very heavily stocked ponds may need to consult with a landscape gardener or other specialist. Just as any others do, outdoor filters must be cleaned and maintained regularly.

DIET

Because most coldwater fish, goldfish and koi in particular, are voracious eaters and will beg for food uninhibitedly, the danger of overfeeding is great. Overfeeding is just as damaging to coldwater environments as it is to tropical aquariums (see *Chapter Ten*)—as a matter of fact, it may cause more trouble because the fish themselves produce much more waste than their tropical cousins. A good general rule to follow is to feed your fish only what they can consume in five minutes. Of course, in an outdoor pond, it can be difficult to know if all of the food has actually been consumed.

All coldwater fish are omnivorous. In their native habitats they are opportunistic feeders and browse on vegetation as well as snatch up any small insects or other live food that they can find. It's a serious mistake to assume that fish kept in an outdoor pond can get enough to eat on their own—the available food in a small, enclosed area is not enough to support the fish.

Coldwater fish require a fairly high amount of carbohydrates in their diet. Flake food makes up a good, basic diet for small goldfish, and larger floating pellets are best for large goldfish, koi, and other fish. Mealworms, bloodworms, freeze-dried plankton, and other live food are excellent supplements. There are also special color-enhancing foods, designed for fancy goldfish that are going to compete in shows.

Both goldfish and koi can be easily "trained," or programmed, to come to a given area at mealtime. In ponds in public areas, such as zoos and botanical gardens, koi become very adept at begging for food from visitors and will stick their entire heads out of the water in an effort to get a handout.

Coldwater fish will eat more when the water gets very warm. If they are left outdoors in the winter they live mostly on the carbohydrates that are stored in their bodies.

Plants

Goldfish and koi are native to still waters in which there is a lot of vegetation, so plants are important to their well-being, whether they live indoors or out. Plants can also help to oxygenate the water in freshwater systems.

When there are good growing conditions in an outdoor setup, the one problem that you may have with your plants is keeping them in check. Floating plants, in particular, can proliferate so quickly that there will soon be little room for the fish. Although the fish will eat duckweed, for instance, they will probably not be able to keep up with its explosive growth.

The most practical method for keeping all nonfloating plants in a container or pond is to pot them and then arrange them as you wish, rather than planting them directly in the bottom material. There are several reasons for this. It allows you to move plants around if you wish and to remove any plants that die or need to be trimmed or divided without disturbing the bottom and making a mess of the water.

Also, if you should ever need to catch any of the fish, your job will be considerably easier if you can remove the plants first.

There are far too many plants that can be used in an outdoor pond or container to mention here, but attractive ornamental water plants are usually a big part of the attraction of outdoor fish keeping. Water lilies are almost always part of an outdoor container or pond setup—their leaves help to provide shade and hiding places for the fish, and the lovely flowers provide aesthetic pleasure. Marsh grasses or reeds make attractive accents, and they are also useful if you want to leave your fish outdoors all winter (see *page 188*). In addition to water lilies, there are a number of other attractive flowering plants that can be grown in the water or at the edge of an outdoor pond. Most of these plants won't survive the winter weather, but must be taken indoors before it gets cold.

Health Problems of Coldwater Fish

Coldwater fish are susceptible to a number of the same diseases that tropicals are, and the treatment for most of these ailments is just the same (see *Chapter Twelve*). It's much more difficult to see fish clearly when they're kept in a large outdoor container or pond than when they're housed in a glass-sided aquarium, and often a disease or illness can go unnoticed for some time. It can be useful to make a point of counting your fish and looking them over as well as possible when you feed them. If a fish doesn't look well, take it out and examine it. In a large pond, one dead fish won't cause a big problem, but in a smaller container it's a good idea to remove the plants and take the carcass out before it begins to decay and foul the water.

Make a partial water change whenever a fish has died or become ill.

Water that gets too cold, too fast, will cause fish to develop *ich*, while the stress from water that is too warm and that contains too little oxygen will lead to *respiratory distress* in coldwater species. If the problem is very bad, fish may jump out of the water in an effort to get more oxygen. In both cases, adjusting the water temperature will remove the cause of the problem. Ich can be treated with appropriate medication, while additional aeration will usually prevent the further loss of fish suffering from a lack of oxygen. *External parasites* are, of course, more apt to attack fish that are kept outdoors. Flukes, anchor worms, and fish lice are all prevalent among outdoor fish. Symptoms and treatment are the same as those described in *Chapter Twelve*.

Fancy goldfish with long, flowing fins and tails are especially subject to *fin rot* and fin damage. Damage is more likely to occur in outdoor situations when the environment contains many objects that can snag or rip fins and tails. Many fancy goldfish breeds have chunky, boxy bodies that are especially prone to *swim bladder problems*, which are often exacerbated by chilling. That's why some of the fancy breeds of goldfish are really not suitable in an outdoor environment, but fare much better in an aquarium setting.

Predators—cats, raccoons, snakes, even alligators in some parts of the country—all pose problems for fish kept in outdoor ponds or containers. Fencing is not much of a deterrent for any of these creatures. A pond with deep enough water may provide sanctuary for fish that are smart enough and quick enough to seek it when a predator appears. This will work for cats and some other mammals, such as possums, which only fish from the bank. Raccoons, however, may go right into the water in an effort to catch a fish, and can pose quite a problem. According to Dr.

Loiselle, many pond-keepers solve the difficulty by offering raccoons more desirable, more easily accessible food. Unless you are sure that there are only one or two raccoons in your vicinity, it doesn't make much sense to try to catch them. Fish-eating snakes and alligators, on the other hand, can sometimes be caught and killed or removed to a distant location.

Insect pests can also pose a problem, and the larvae of some insects, such as dragonflies and some moths, may prey on small fish. Other than removing the adults when you see them, there is little that you can do to control these insects. Chemical insecticides are poisonous to fish, and most gardeners are loath to destroy dragonflies in any event, because they are so beneficial.

Some Coldwater Freshwater Fish

Dr. Loiselle reminds people that, if fish are going to be kept outdoors, they should be interesting and attractive to look at from above. That's why brightly colored fish such as goldfish and koi have always been so popular for ponds and outdoor containers. *Goldfish* are by far the most well-known of all aquarium fish. They have been around since the tenth century, and many, many varieties have been developed through breeding. The most often seen colors are the familiar orange, white, black, and speckled. Goldfish belong to the cyprinid family, and inhabit still, nontropical waters with lots of vegetation. They are hardy, peaceful, and undemanding schooling fish and the larger, plainer varieties can be kept successfully with other large coldwater fish. Under ideal conditions, goldfish can live to be 25 years old.

There are far too many types to name here, but the most common are:

- Plain, single-tailed, short-finned, "common" goldfish, usually orange-colored
- Double-tailed goldfish with veil-tails, fantails, and fringe-tails—these fish can injure their tails and fins easily and are not as suitable for outdoor living as the common goldfish
- "Headgrowth" goldfish, such as lionheads, orandas, and ranchus, all have exaggerated, hoodlike, brightly colored growths surrounding their heads. Many have no dorsal fins. These fish require excellent water quality because the flow of water through their gills may be impeded by the headgrowth. The short-bodied species, such as the ranchu, are poor swimmers and often suffer from swim-bladder problems

The "eye" breeds all have been developed with strangely shaped eyes. All are subject to eye damage in varying degrees. *Telescopes* have protruding eyes and short, round bodies (this makes them susceptible to swim-bladder problems)—the most common of these is the *black moor*. *Celestials'* eyes turn upward, which make it very difficult for them to see and to feed—they should not be kept in a mixed aquarium for this reason. Bubble-eyed goldfish have large, fluid-filled sacs protruding to the side, underneath their eyes—they, too, have difficulty seeing well, and the fluid sacs are very delicate. In general, none of the "eye" goldfish do well outdoors because of the danger of damage and chilling.

Koi, colored carp, or *nishiki goi* (*in Japanese*) are also cyprinids, and are similar in body shape to the common goldfish, except that they grow much, much larger—up to three feet in length, and they have a pair of barbels at their mouth corners. Dr. Loiselle points out that koi were mentioned in Japanese writings as early as the sixth century A.D.

195

They are very hardy, and only young fish are suitable for an indoor aquarium because of their size. Koi come in a wide variety of colors, the most simple division of which are one-color, two-color, three-color, with metallic and non-metallic scales. Fancy showfish koi can be very expensive, retailing for tens of thousands of dollars by mail order! They are extremely long-lived, and may live to be a hundred or more years old.

OTHER FISH

Bitterlings are also cyprinids. Minnowlike and silvery, they are peaceful fish that grow to be about three-and-a-half inches long. They can be wintered outdoors. They have an unusual method of spawning. They lay their eggs inside of a live freshwater mussel. During spawning, male bitterlings assume a brilliant violet-green color. Bitterlings are hardy, relatively disease-free, and omnivorous.

White Cloud Mountain Minnows are hardy little (up to an inch-and-a-half) cyprinids that naturally inhabit subtropical mountain streams in which the water is about 60° to 70° on average. They are lively, schooling fish that should be kept in groups of six or more. There are other kinds of minnows, including native American *shiners* that are hardy and make good pond fish. Various kinds of *dwarf sunfish* can be excellent colorful pond inhabitants and can withstand water temperatures as low as the high forties.

Guppies, platys, and mollies like cooler water than most tropicals do, and can all be kept outdoors as long as the water doesn't go much below 65°, at which point they'll begin to die off.

There are a number of other kinds of fish that will do well in a coldwater aquarium and/or an outdoor container or pond.

Collecting Your Own Fish

It can be fun to collect your own fish, especially for an outdoor pool. Native fish can be very attractive and they will be hardy, resistant to disease, and wily when it comes to avoiding predators.

However, you do have to be careful. It's illegal to capture some native fish, especially endangered species and so-called "sport" fish. So, before you set out to bring some pretty fish home, find out what their legal status is by calling your state or local Fish and Game Department. If you do capture any native fish to stock your pool and want to re-lease them in the fall, be absolutely sure that you put them back into the same waters that they came from in order to avoid upsetting the balance of nature.

It's usually not a good idea to mix native, wild fish in the same pond with valuable ornamentals. Not only may they be carrying a disease organism to which they, but not your pets, are immune, but they might also be stronger and more aggressive than domestically raised fish and could cause a serious problem.

14

Saltwater (Marine) Fish

Up until recent years, the difficulty and expense of marine fish keeping made it prohibitive for the average person to pursue. It was a hobby reserved for very dedicated, very wealthy enthusiasts.

Nowadays, although it is still more expensive to set up and stock a saltwater aquarium than a freshwater tank, safer, better methods of collecting and transporting specimens and modern techniques and equipment have been developed that make it possible for almost anyone to keep a marine aquarium. Nevertheless, most experts agree that it is usually best to begin with a freshwater aquarium in order to get your ''sea legs'' before investing in a more expensive marine setup.

As I said in the previous chapter on coldwater fish keeping, there is not space in this book to describe a very complex subject fully, but here are some general highlights about marine fish keeping.

According to all of the experts, the single biggest problem that people have with saltwater aquariums stems from a lack of sufficient *patience*. As he/she does with any fish aquarium, an eager potential fish owner must take enough time to season the tank properly before introducing the inhabitants, but this takes even more time with saltwater aquariums because desirable water qualities fall into a very narrow spectrum.

The rule of thumb mentioned in the chapter on aquariums—that the larger the tank, the easier it is to maintain proper water conditions—is particularly true for marine tanks. Experts agree that the smallest viable size for a marine aquarium is 30 gallons, and that the largest tank that you can afford is the best assurance for success in marine fish keeping.

Running-in the Aquarium

A **run-in**, or "seasoning," period is more crucial for saltwater setups than for fresh because sea creatures are much more sensitive to changes in the water chemistry than freshwater fish are, so the tank must be stable before valuable inhabitants are introduced. Reef inhabitants, especially, are used to environmental stability. But it takes longer to season a saltwater tank—up to eight weeks—that's where the patience comes in! As in a freshwater setup, it is also important not to overload the tank right away, but to add the fish and/or invertebrates gradually, to allow the filtering system to adjust to each new inhabitant without becoming overloaded. It's also prudent not to add rare or valuable specimens to the tank until you're sure that all is well.

Marine systems are "a lot like old cars—they get better as they age," according to Daniel Bebak. Just as Dr. Loiselle does for freshwater tanks, he recommends putting a few hardy fish in the tank to start the biological cycle. Damselfish are very tolerant of poor water conditions, and a lot of fish stores will actually "loan" a beginning marine fish keeper some damsels to start a tank with. After a month or two, once the biological cycle is up and running, the store will either take back the damsels or sell them to the fish keeper if he wants to keep them. Sailfin mollies are also often used to start up marine tanks, as are clownfish. If you are lucky enough to live near a seacoast, you can sometimes collect some small, hardy fish such as pinfish, use them to cycle the tank with, and then return them to the water from which they came.

Water

As opposed to freshwater fish, most tropical saltwater animals come from water that is similar, whether they originate in the Atlantic, Pacific, Indian, or Caribbean Oceans. Natural seawater varies a good deal less than fresh water that can come from completely different environments, ranging from fresh, swiftly flowing mountain streams to virtually motionless or stagnant ponds in which little fresh water ever flows. For this reason, it is both easier and more difficult to maintain the proper water qualities for saltwater fish and invertebrates than for freshwater fish.

It is easier because there is little variation in the demands of various species of fish—you can always know exactly what the ideal water conditions are. It is more difficult because the parameters within which the water quality must be maintained are more precise.

Natural seawater is, of course, hard. It has a pH of around 8.2, so the ideal level of pH for tropical marine fish falls in a very narrow range, between 8.0 and 8.3. According to Dan Bebak, "Once you get below 8.0, you've got a problem. Higher, into the mid-8's, is better."

Synthetic seawater comes in premeasured bags to suit the size of an aquarium. It is simply dissolved in fresh water to the desired density. The density, or salinity, of seawater is measured in terms of its *specific gravity*, which compares the density of the water to that of distilled water. This is measured with an instrument called a *hydrometer*, a sealed glass tube that is weighted at one end so that it can float in the water. The average specific gravity for a marine aquarium should be about 1.023 and can be altered by either adding more fresh water or more salt. The salinity of the water will increase with evaporation and it may be necessary to top the tank off with fresh water from time to time, especially in warm or very dry climates.

The *trace elements* found in natural seawater are very important for the health of all sea creatures, especially invertebrates. That's why it's very important for the success of a marine tank to add supplementary trace elements in the form of commercially available mixtures, or to perform frequent *water changes* (trace elements are contained in all of the seawater mixes that are on the market). Daniel Bebak recommends that you change 10 to 15 percent of the water in the average marine aquarium at least once a month—more often if the tank is very crowded. "The minute that you add a small crab or two, for instance, to a tank full of fish, you have a lot more demand for trace elements because crabs require enormous amounts of specific trace elements to help strengthen their shells." When you do change the water in the tank, it's best to take the old water from the bottom with a siphon or gravel cleaner in order to get rid of accumulated wastes and gas pockets.

Ammonia buildup is also an enemy of saltwater fish and invertebrates, and regular testing can help to prevent this from happening. However, the most important ways to avoid unnecessary ammonia from accumulating are to be sure not to overstock your aquarium (one rule is to allow one gallon of water per half-inch of livestock), and to make sure to wait for enough time before introducing fish and/or invertebrates to the aquarium.

Filters for Saltwater Aquariums

Undergravel, biological filtration is a must for marine aquariums in order to develop the correct biological cycle. At least two inches of substrate on top of the filter is necessary in order for it to work correctly. In marine aquariums, *crushed coral* or *crushed shell*, rather than gravel, are used as substrates. Because of their buffering qualities, these mediums can help to keep the pH of the water up to the correct levels.

If an aquarium is much larger than 30 gallons, Dan Bebak recommends using reverse-flow undergravel filtration with an outside power filter. This method helps to prevent the substrate from becoming packed down and keeps it clean and free of debris. Power heads are often used in marine tanks because they increase the flow of water in the tank, and invertebrates like very strong, wavelike water currents.

Recently, some very advanced methods of filtration and water treatment for marine aquariums have appeared on the market. Among them are ultraviolet sterilization, wet/dry filter systems, and protein skimmers. Some experts advocate their use by all amateur marine fish keepers, but Daniel Bebak is "not 100 percent sold on their effectiveness for the average person. The only time that I've seen these systems used to their fullest potential is in huge commercial setups. I've seen them used quite successfully by major fish importers who are moving large numbers of fish in and out of their tanks and pulling hundreds of thousands of gallons of water an hour through their filters.'' In his opinion, a good undergravel filter is all that's necessary for most home aquariums.

Other Equipment

Submersible heaters, thermometers, and any other equipment that's going to be used in the tank should be specifically designed for use in saltwater in order to avoid corrosion. Tropical marine fish like a water temperature of 76° to 78° F.

While normal fluorescent lights will do for a marine aquarium, many fanciers prefer to use *actinic* lights. These lights are expensive, but they have a very strong ultraviolet spectrum that is very good for invertebrates and helps promote the growth of beneficial algae.

Plants and Furnishings

Live plants are not recommended for marine aquariums. As Daniel Bebak says, ''If plants are hard to maintain in a freshwater setup, they're twice as difficult in a marine tank. The fish will eat them, and the plants will die and disintegrate, making it much harder to maintain the water quality.'' There are now artificial marine plants that are very attractive.

Rocks, shells, dead corals, and other appropriate decorations that might naturally appear in seawater are all excellent furnishings for a marine aquarium. Don't ever use self-collected materials because they can introduce all sorts of undesirable organisms into the tank. Already seasoned furnishings of all kinds are available in most fish stores.

Most marine fish appreciate nooks and crannies to hide in, and it's essential for some species, such as moray eels, to have someplace to hide.

Diet

Most inhabitants of the sea are omnivorous and must be fed a variety of foods in captivity. Many marine fish have quite small mouths and all of their food should be minced or chopped into small pieces.

Small fish should be given appropriate flake food supplemented by frozen brine shrimp, worms, or other protein sources. Predatory fish such as lionfish, triggerfish, or moray eels like live food. "Feeder" fish—guppies and small goldfish—are sold in most pet stores. Be very sure that any feeder fish you choose are healthy. At Mote Marine Science Aquarium, they prefer not to feed their carnivores live fish, but to give them cleaned, frozen large shrimp and sardines instead. One reason for this is that it would be impossible to raise and maintain enough live feeder fish for their large carnivorous population. Other considerations are the ever-present danger of introducing disease organisms via live feedings, and the large amount of waste (of scales, etc.) that's left behind when live feeders are consumed. Most of these concerns are not applicable to a person who owns just one lionfish, for instance. However, for convenience sake, you might want to train your carnivorous fish to accept killed food or pieces of meat for at least some of its feedings. If you start out when the fish is young, you may have no difficulty getting it to eat the food you offer, but if the fish is stubborn, you might try an old trick to fool it into taking killed food.

Impale the food on the end of a long broom straw and wiggle it around in front of the fish. If you're lucky, the fish will think that the food is alive and grab it. After several feedings, once the fish gets used to the taste of the food, you may be able to simply drop a serving into the tank without using the wiggling ruse.

Special care must be taken to be sure that slow movers, such as seahorses, pipefish, and blennies, are able to get enough food. Brine shrimp and other food should be given directly to these animals so that they can find it readily. In general, these shy fish should not be kept with more aggressive individuals because they won't compete for food and will soon go hungry.

Invertebrates require brine shrimp, blood worms, and chopped fish or clams. The food should be dropped on or very near them. Tubeworms and some other invertebrates live on algae and other tiny microorganisms in the water. They are best kept in an invertebrate-only tank in which the filtration is not strong enough to remove these small organisms from the water. Hermit crabs are good scavengers and will consume any uneaten food from the bottom of a community tank.

Diseases of Saltwater Fish—Treatment and Prevention

Although marine fish can live a long time—years and years, these fish are subject to many of the same illnesses that freshwater fish are. *Stress* due to overcrowding, poor water conditions, diet, or undue upsets from moving and outside agitation is again the primary reason for an outbreak of disease. The major illness that they suffer from is a marine form of *ich* (see *Chapter Twelve*). They also are prone to various kinds of *fungal infections*.

Although there are a number of very effective medications on the market for these diseases, *copper* is the primary ingredient in most of them. Copper is poisonous to all invertebrates so, unless it is only present in minute traces, either the invertebrates must be removed from the tank before it is treated, or the fish must be removed to a hospital tank for treatment. If the main tank is treated with a copper-based medication, an activated carbon filter will help to remove it from the water when the treatment is over. But, before returning the invertebrates to the tank, all furnishings must be thoroughly cleaned to remove any copper residue, and the water should be tested for any traces of copper—there are special test kits available for this purpose.

Because marine fish do drink water, antibiotic medications in solution may help them if they have a systemic bacterial illness. Care must be taken when antibiotics are used that they are not strong enough to destroy the bacteria in the biological filtration system. Again, the use of a hospital tank will help to prevent problems in the main aquarium.

Marine tangs are especially susceptible to *lateral-line disease*, a stress-related fungal infestation in which the fish develop white patches down their sides and suffer from fin loss and anorexia. At Mote Marine they found that isolating their tangs in a sheltered hospital tank and feeding them medicated flake food reduced stress sufficiently so that the fish began to recover nicely. Other fish keepers with similar problems have found that home remedies work, which goes to prove what many fish keepers have known all along—that fish medicine is still a very inexact science.

PREVENTING ILLNESS

Quarantine of any new stock will help to prevent disease outbreaks, but Dan Bebak feels that it is not as essential for an individual fish buyer of marines as it is for freshwater fish. He reasons that, because the turnover in marine fish is a lot slower than it is for freshwater varieties (due to their considerably greater cost), an individual fish will usually have been living in either a wholesaler's or fish dealer's tank for some time before it is purchased and will, therefore, have already been effectively quarantined. That is, if the stress of capture, handling, and shipment hasn't caused any recessive diseases or disorders to surface by the time a potential buyer looks at it, it's probably OK.

Many fish dealers now have a very good system in use. They label a tank with a sign: *"Speckled grouper. Arrived in store on December 11. Eating well."* This is very useful for the consumer, who can come in, see that a fish has been in the shop for a month, looks fine and is eating well, and therefore is safe to buy. Whereas, if a fish has only been in the shop for three days, an informed customer will know enough to wait for a while before purchasing the fish.

To prevent serious shock, it is very important to acclimate a marine fish to the water in your aquarium before you dump it in. See *Chapter Nine* on how to do this.

Fish For a Marine Aquarium

Dan Bebak divides marine fish into two categories: ''the pickers and the swallowers.'' Many marine fish are extremely territorial and aggressive, even with their own kind, and care must be taken not to inadvertently mix any very nasty individuals or there will be a lot of badly nipped fins and tails. Others, such as lionfish, will eat any individual that they can, so their tank-mates must be chosen very carefully.

There are far too many kinds of marine fish to even begin to list them all here. In addition to lionfish, other predatory species include moray eels and groupers, all of which can get along well together or with larger fish and make excellent pets. Each of these fish is solitary and territorial and does not like others of its own kind.

Damselfish are a lot like freshwater cichlids in their intense territoriality, and will pick on other fish and nag them incessantly, unless the others are larger than they are, such as groupers or morays. They do sometimes get along all right with marine angelfish. Triggerfish can also be aggressive and picky with other fish—some varieties are so vicious that they cannot be kept with any other fish. Marine angelfish and butterflyfish are usually territorial, and most kinds must be kept singly although there are some varieties that form compatible pairs.

Many clownfish are unusual among marines in that they have been raised in captivity. Also known as anemone fish because of their unusual symbiotic relationship with poisonous sea anemones, clownfish are cute and rather pugnacious for their size and will protect their territory (anemone) vigorously. Each clownfish in an aquarium must have its own anemone to be happy.

Yellow tangs, or surgeonfish, are an exception to the behavior of most marines in that they do school and can be kept in small groups. They are quite hardy vegetarian fish and like to eat algae, lettuce, and other greens.

Among the peaceful marines are the gentle seahorses and pipefish that do best in species-specific tanks or with invertebrates. The only problem with this mix is that these fish prefer calm waters while most invertebrates like a lot of water motion.

Invertebrates

There are many different kinds of invertebrates that are suitable for a marine aquarium, either along with fish or alone. Many people find invertebrates so fascinating that the popularity of "reef aquariums"—that attempt to create an entire live, self-contained ecosystem—has grown by leaps and bounds. Care must be taken when mixing fish with invertebrates because predatory fish, such as triggerfish, feed on mollusks and other invertebrates. Starfish, among the invertebrates, are also predatory and will eat mollusks, small fish, and other starfish.

Popular invertebrates include *crustaceans*, such as crabs, shrimps, and so forth, which are generally peaceful and make good tank-mates for fish. Anemones come in a wide variety of shapes and colors—some can be difficult to keep successfully. Brittle stars, sea urchins, and sea cucumbers all belong to the same family as starfish, but they are generally not predatory and will feed mostly on algae and detritus in the tank. Clams, scallops, cowries, and other mollusks can all make attractive additions to a marine setup. Some snails, on the other hand, are predatory. Marine *worms* like tubeworms and featherdusters are attractive, harmless filter-feeders that are not preyed on in general.

As you can see, the entire area of invertebrates for aquariums is a very complex one, and it will pay to do some research before choosing any of them for your own aquarium.

Coldwater Marines

People who live on seacoasts often collect their own marine specimens to keep in aquariums. Depending on the area, anemones, starfish, various mollusks, crustaceans, and small fish can be collected in tidepools and at the shoreline. Most marine species are not endangered and are not, therefore, protected by fish-and-game laws, but it is a good idea to check with a local aquarium or fish keeping society to find out what the rules and laws are, if any, about keeping fish and other sea creatures in captivity.

Before you set out to collect specimens for your tank you should have an aquarium set up, seasoned, and ready for the newcomers so that they won't be too shocked by the transition from the sea. You will need an appropriate filter, lighting, and other equipment in order to maintain your "catch" healthily. Tank furnishings such as rocks and shells can be collected along with your live specimens. You won't want to lug water from the shore to your house, so it's best to use artificial seawater mix. In many areas, you may need to chill the water in order to keep your animals healthy—the temperature of seawater is usually a lot cooler than "room temperature." There are commercially available chillers available for this purpose.

One of the advantages of collecting specimens is that, if your charges should not seem to fare too well, get into serious arguments with each other, or grow too big for the aquarium, you can always take them back to where you found them and release them, knowing that they will probably do very well.

Children, especially, can really learn a lot from catching, caring for, and eventually releasing sea creatures. This is, by far, a better learning experience for them than collecting live seashore specimens and allowing them to die and dry out for display.

Where Do They Come From?

Very few ornamental tropical marine fish are raised on fish farms in this country. This is a shame, because tank-raised animals are better-adjusted, healthier, and cheaper in the long run than those that are wild-caught. It stands to reason that by avoiding the stress and shock of capture, shipping, and handling, tank-bred fish would be several steps ahead of wild-caught fish in their ability to withstand illness. With the tremendous growth in the popularity of marine aquariums, there will hopefully soon be more fish and invertebrates grown and raised domestically.

In recent years there has been a lot of publicity about the use of cyanide to capture tropical marine fish for the retail market. Although it is illegal, sodium cyanide is apparently still used in the Philippines. In the March 1989 issue of *Audubon* magazine, an article entitled "State of the Reef," by Kenneth Brower, contains the following description: "The aquarium-fish collectors are poor men . . . carrying small detergent bottles refilled with sodium cyanide. The divers call the chemical 'magic.' A squirt into the coral, and all the fish hiding there come out spinning and jerking . . . for every fish captured alive by cyanide, nine die. . . ." Not only does it stun fish, making them easier to capture, but cyanide also enhances their color temporarily, so that they are more attractive to potential buyers—although many of these fish are so badly damaged that they will die prematurely after purchase. A devastating side effect of cyanide use is that it kills live coral and other marine invertebrates. According to an article in the Spring 1989

211

issue of *Focus*, published by the World Wildlife Fund, The International Marine Life Alliance (IMA) has waged a publicity campaign to make pet wholesalers and retailers aware of this problem and urged them to purchase only fish that are captured in nets without the use of chemicals, as they are in Hawaii and Guam.

Daniel Bebak feels that the campaign launched by IMA and other concerned organizations has worked. Most wholesalers no longer buy cyanide-caught fish because they can't sell them to informed retail dealers—not only because of ecological concerns, but because the poisoned fish so often die soon after purchase. This is one more reason why it's always advisable to purchase livestock from a responsible, reliable dealer and to ask questions about their origin before you buy any expensive marines.

PART SEVEN

Additional Fish-Keeping Concerns

15

Breeding and Showing Aquarium Fish

Once they're well established in successful fish keeping, many people want to go one step further in the hobby and try their hands at breeding fish. Some breed fish just for the fun of it, others become intrigued with the genetics of breeding and strive to develop better and more colorful specimens of fish.

If they are especially successful at breeding and raising beautiful fish that they want to share with other enthusiasts, the next step is to enter one of the many shows that are run by fish-keeping societies all over the United States.

Encouraging Spawning

It can be difficult to sex some freshwater fish and some experience may be necessary to select a breeding pair. Mature female fish carry unfertilized eggs inside their bodies all of the time and can often be identified by their swollen bellies. Color, size, and fin differences can also help you to make a differentiation between sexes in some species. Except for cichlids, which form their own pairs, most freshwater fish will accept whatever mate is introduced into an aquarium.

If you are selecting a pair of fish with breeding in mind, you will want to pay particular attention to good body conformation and color. Because of the very distinct possibility that eggs and/or fry will be eaten by other tank inhabitants in a community tank, many people advocate placing a breeding pair in a separate aquarium. Some parents can be allowed to stay with their young, but the egg-scatterers (see *page 217*) should be removed as soon as the eggs are fertilized or they may eat them. In many cases, both parents help to guard both eggs and fry, but male bettas, for instance, will fight with the female as soon as the eggs are laid and she should be removed for her own safety.

Appropriate furnishings—e.g., flowerpots or tiles for egg-depositing cichlids and feathery plants for the young of livebearers—are necessary for successful spawning. Killifish and others that lay eggs that adhere to surfaces appreciate artificial spawning "mops" made of wool or other material to lay their eggs on.

Water and diet also play an important part in conditioning fish for successful spawning. Obviously, a fish that has a very nutritious diet will be in better condition than one that is poorly fed. Good water conditions are essential, and some fish are encouraged to spawn by water that is warmer than usual.

There are a number of other specific steps that can be taken in order to encourage successful spawning in various kinds of fish. If you are really serious about breeding fish, talk to as many experienced people as possible before you begin.

Breeding Methods of Fish

Saltwater fish rarely breed in a household aquarium, although they do breed in captivity when they are kept in huge facilities such as Living Seas in Orlando, Florida.

The average freshwater fish owner, however, will often become a breeder inadvertently, although the resulting eggs or fry will probably not survive, but will make a delicious surprise meal for the other tank inhabitants. Successful fish-breeding requires some knowledge of different breeding methods and habits. Here is a very brief overview of breeding methods.

LIVEBEARERS

Livebearing fish differ from others in that the fry appear, fully developed, from the female's body. The male introduces sperm directly into the female with a specially modified anal fin. After the eggs have been fertilized, the fry develop in a month or two, after which they are born, fully formed and able to swim quickly away to find shelter.

EGG-LAYERS

All other fish are egg-layers and the eggs are fertilized by the male outside of the female's body. They are laid in different ways and in different places, according to the species of fish.

Some fish simply scatter their eggs and take no further care of them. In fact, they often eat their own eggs. Danios, barbs, goldfish, and some characins are egg-scatterers.

Cichlids and catfish are the most well-known of the fish that carefully place their fertilized eggs on a preselected site such as a flowerpot or large leaf. They will then guard the

217

eggs and fan them to help keep fresh water flowing over them, and take care of and feed newly hatched fry. These fish are known as *egg-depositors*.

Some cichlids and bettas carry the fertilized eggs in their mouths until they are ready to hatch and will often open their mouths at the first sign of danger so that newly hatched fry can swim in for protection. During the time that she's carrying the eggs, the female is unable to eat.

Other fish, such as killifish, bury their eggs in the substrate. In the wild, adult killifish will die during the dry season and never see their fry.

Anabantids, such as bettas and many gouramis, are well-known as bubble-nest builders. The males construct a nest of bubbles into which the fertilized eggs are laid and are usually guarded by the male until hatching.

Raising Fry

This, too, is a complex subject and requires knowledge of the specific needs of various species of fish. In general, fry are very delicate. In a natural setting a very small percentage of fry actually grow up to adulthood, so you shouldn't feel too bad if you lose some fry. As a matter of fact, most experts advise that you discard any fry that are not vigorous and healthy right away. The first few days are the most critical and, once the fry are swimming freely, they will need to be fed. Except for young cichlids, who are fed by their parents at first, most fry will relish special liquid fry diets. Good lighting will encourage fry to eat.

It's always a good idea to keep notes about your breeding experiences for future reference.

Showing Fish

Fish shows occur all over the country all year long—a glance at a fish-keeping magazine will give you schedules. If you belong to any of the many fish-keeping societies you will probably know all about fish shows.

Just as with any other kind of pet or hobby, shows vary from local to regional and national. They can be specialty shows that concentrate on only one kind of fish, or more general shows in which all kinds of fish are welcome.

Fish are either exhibited singly in bare tanks, or in groups in completely furnished aquariums. Experienced owners who exhibit fish regularly know exactly on what basis fish and aquariums are judged. They also know just how to prepare their fish so that they will show off to their best advantage. Proper conditioning and preparation are a must before attempting to show one or several fish.

Transporting and showing fish is not something that should be undertaken by a novice fish keeper. If you think that you might be interested in showing your fish at some future date, the best way to prepare is to visit a number of shows, talk to other exhibitors, and ask a lot of questions.

Catching and Transporting Fish

Whether you are taking one or more fish to a show, are moving, or simply going to the veterinarian, you need to know how to minimize the trauma of capture and travel for your fish.

One of the best ways to catch a fish without damaging its scales and osmotic barrier is to use a plastic bag instead of a net. Michael Stoskopf describes how to do this: there are two methods. You can make tiny holes in the end of a bag for the water to flow through and then pour the fish into one without holes once it's captured; or, you can simply use an intact bag to catch the fish in. The second method may be a little bit more difficult the first time that you try it because a water-filled bag is not as maleable as an empty one is. Whichever kind of bag you use, put it into the water and hold it there. At first, the fish will probably panic. After a while, however, they will calm down a bit. Then put your other hand in the other corner of the tank. The fish will immediately swim away from your hand and into the bag. Once you've caught the fish, it's always a good idea to use two bags nested together for safety sake. When the fish is safely in the bag, it can be sealed, leaving an air space on top. If the fish is going to be traveling further or longer than a short trip to the veterinarian's or around the corner to a show, pure oxygen must be pumped in to replace the air in the bag.

If the weather is neither too warm nor too cold and the trip short, the plastic bag can be placed directly into a paper bag to protect the fish from the fright while traveling from place to place. In most conditions, however, the fish must be protected from chilling (or overheating) because the small amount of water in a plastic bag will rapidly calibrate with the outside temperature. Commercial fish shippers use styrofoam shipping boxes into which they place the plastic-bagged fish to insulate them from temperature fluctuations. If you don't happen to have a styrofoam shipping box, an insulated beverage cooler or picnic carrier will do to keep the fish comfortable for an hour or two.

16

Moving With Fish/
Care of Fish
When You're Away

People who own fish can't always avoid moving, nor can they always arrange to be home to take care of their pets every single day.

Moving With Fish

Moving your fish to a different home needn't be a serious trauma as long as you prepare ahead of time. I can still remember many years ago when I was a child and my father had a tropical aquarium. We were going to go away for the whole summer and he decided to take the fish with us. Tropical aquarium fish keeping was then a relatively new hobby, and no one could offer much advice about how to transport the fish, so he decided to simply take out the plants and furnishings, disconnect the filter and pump, remove half of the water, and leave the fish in the tank for the car trip. We drove for about five hours with the poor fish sloshing and bumping around in the half-filled aquarium and, as soon as we arrived at our destination, the first thing that we had to do before even unloading the car was to set the aquarium up with its filter and pump and refill it—I don't remember whether or not we used seasoned water or not. Surprisingly, about half of the fish survived their bumpy journey, but on the way home the next fall most of them succumbed.

This method of transporting fish is definitely not recommended. Instead, the fish should be caught and put into appropriate containers either singly or in pairs, as described in *Chapter Fifteen*. If the trip is a long one, you should check on the fish from time to time to be sure that they're all right. If it's either very hot or very cold, feel the outsides of the plastic bags from time to time. If you have a supply of gaseous oxygen with you, you can open each bag and adjust the temperature with fresh water and refill it with oxygen before sealing. If you don't have any replacement oxygen along, you'll have to cool or heat the water from outside the bag. Some people advocate treating the water in which the fish will be traveling with a small amount of salt or a mild antibiotic in case the fish are bruised from capture or travel. Fish should not be fed during travel—they probably wouldn't eat anyway. If possible, in addition to the water in the bags, take enough "old" water from your aquarium in jugs or bottles so that you can fill it halfway when you arrive at your destination. Don't wash your old filter mediums and gravel, but put them into plastic bags so that they remain moist and retain their bacterial load. Plants and other aquarium furnishing should be rinsed. Plants can be transported in tightly sealed plastic bags with a little water in them.

The aquarium itself should be rinsed and wrapped carefully. You can put wrapped equipment such as lights, heater, and thermometer into the tank for transport.

Once you arrive at your destination, you'll have to find a suitable spot for the aquarium and set it up right away. The same steps that you used when setting it up originally should be followed (this is another situation in which notes come in handy), and the fish should be carefully acclimated to the water before being dumped into the tank. At first the fish may be nervous and upset, as well they might be, but once they locate old hiding places and favorite nooks and crannies in their "new" tank, they'll settle down and begin to feed again.

If the water chemistry is very different in your new home than it was before, you may have to experiment a bit to reach the proper treatments and proportions. Until you do, test the water daily.

A few losses are to be expected if you've made a big move with your fish but, hopefully, if you've planned well and taken appropriate care, your losses won't be too great.

Care of Fish When You're Away

Whether you simply have a nice community tank of fish that you are fond of or are a serious hobbyist, one of the things that you should think about is—what to do with your fish when you aren't there to look after them? In the best of all possible worlds we would all have knowledgeable, caring people to look after our pets when we go away on business or vacation. Unfortunately, this is not the case and it's not even possible to take your fish to a boarding kennel or pet store to be looked after.

Aquarium fish cannot be left without food for more than two or three days and, unfortunately, well-meaning but inexperienced friends can often do more harm than good when it comes to feeding fish. There are "vacation fish foods" on the market that are designed to provide food for various lengths of time, from a weekend to ten days. They are blocks that dissolve in the water and release food slowly.

However, Ken Stassfield warns that they can "mess up the water very badly," and that at least a 20 percent water change is necessary after they are used. They cannot be used in marine tanks, but there are automatic, timed flake-food feeders that can be used in both salt- and freshwater aquariums for various periods of time, depending on their size. They can be set to dispense different amounts of food once or twice a day and should be pretested before you go away to be sure that they are working right and giving out the correct amount of food. However, these feeders do no good for fish that require live food.

Lights can also be timed automatically, and there are even devices on the market that will run all of the aquarium equipment at preprogrammed intervals.

As good as all of these devices may be, they cannot maintain a tank at a peak level for very long. Water changes and cleaning are still tasks that must be performed regularly by human hands. The best solution if you are going to be away for any length of time is still to find someone who can look after your aquarium in your absence.

Rather than depending on volunteer help from friends or relatives, it's best to pay someone to do this. It will put the job on a professional basis and not only serve to make the caretaker more responsible, but will make it easier for you to ask for extra, special tasks to be performed when needed. If you belong to an aquarium association, perhaps there is a member or a member's youngster who would be willing to serve as a fish "sitter." Barring this, your fish dealer may have a knowledgeable student or other part-time employee who would be happy to earn some extra money in the evenings or on Sundays. Be sure to have your fish sitter visit well ahead of your expected absence and watch you as you take care of your aquarium—because everyone does things a little bit differently. No matter how knowledgeable the sitter may be, always write out clear, detailed instructions. Don't be afraid of offending the sitter—most will welcome a checklist to work with as a reminder.

If you do have automatic equipment, a visit twice a week or even weekly to check the animals and equipment will probably be sufficient, combined with longer visits once a month or more to change water and clean the tank.

Behavioral Characteristics of Some Popular Freshwater Tropical Fish

FISH	Activity Level	Compati-bility	Usual Tank Level	Charac-teristics/ Special Needs
ANABANTIDS (also called Labyrinth Fishes; from Asia and Africa)				
Betta Splendens Siamese Fighting Fish	Slow-swimming	Very pugnacious with other males; species tank	All levels; may breathe at surface	Plants; bubble-nest builder
Gourami Many sizes (Dwarf, Honey, Kissing, Lace, Moonlight)	Slow-swimming	Generally peaceful, but may be aggressive when breeding; community tank with similar-sized fishes; kissing gourami may suck on other fishes	All levels; may breathe at surface	Floating plants; some are timid/shy; most are bubble-nest builders

FISH	Activity Level	Compatibility	Usual Tank Level	Characteristics/ Special Needs
Paradise-fish	Moderately active	Very aggressive; species tank; or community with other tough fish	All levels; may breathe at surface	Plants; bubble-nest builder; cool water
Perch, climbing	Moderately active	Peaceful, but predatory; keep with other large fish.	All levels; may breathe at surface, and climb out of the water	Plants; hiding places; bubble-nest builder

CATFISH (several families)

SOUTH AMERICAN CATFISH

Banjo	Active; digs	Peaceful	Bottom	Nocturnal; buries itself
Dwarf Armored (Black-spotted, Bronze, Elegant, Emerald, Leopard, Peppered)	Active; may hide in daylight	Peaceful; good in a community tank	Lower levels; may gulp air at surface	Schooling; usually happiest in small groups; most are nocturnal
Naked (Bumblebee, Graceful, Spotted-Pim)	Usually active; older fish may get lazy	Predatory toward smaller fish	Bottom	Schooling; may be timid; nocturnal

FISH	Activity Level	Compati- bility	Usual Tank Level	Charac- teristics/ Special Needs
Sucker- mouth (Bristle- nosed, or Bristle- mouth, Pep- pered, Plecs)	Tends to attach to things	Generally peaceful; some may be territorial toward other cat- fish; may suck on other fish	All levels	Happier in small groups; will destroy soft plants
Talking (Spiny)	Lethargic	Safe with other same- sized fish, may be ter- ritorial with other catfish	Lower; may gulp air if oxygen level is low	Nocturnal, shy; need hiding places

AFRICAN AND ASIAN CATFISH

FISH	Activity Level	Compati- bility	Usual Tank Level	Charac- teristics/ Special Needs
Bagrid, or Bumblebee (Bumble- bee, Dwarf Bagrid, One-spot, Two-spot)	Active	Adults may be preda- tory toward smaller fish	Midwater and bottom; some upside- down	Nocturnal; some shy; some schooling
Glass	Constant, slow swim- mers	Peaceful; good in community tank, but not with fast swim- mers	Mid to up- per levels	Schooling, need com- panionship; diurnal
Upside- down (Clown, Polka-dot or Angel)	May be boisterous and disrup- tive	Territorial, but safe with other fish; young and/or small OK in com- munity tank	Many swim upside- down	Live in groups; may be shy; noc- turnal

229

FISH	Activity Level	Compatibility	Usual Tank Level	Characteristics/ Special Needs

CHARACINS *and Related Families* (many diverse families, most from South and Central America, Texas; some from Africa)

FISH	Activity Level	Compatibility	Usual Tank Level	Characteristics/ Special Needs
Hatchetfish	Lively, gliding	Very peaceful; keep with small, lower-level swimmers	Upper; will jump out of water	Schooling; shy
Headstanders	Often rest with head down	Compatible with same-sized fish	Swim at all levels; feed on bottom	Schooling; need hiding places
Pencilfish	Lively; rest and dart	Community tank with other small fish	Mid and upper levels	Schooling; may be timid at first
Tetras (Bleeding Heart, Cardinal, Diamond, Emperor, Neon)	Lively, active	Community tank	Mid and lower levels	Must be kept in schools
Others				
Blind Cave Fish	Lively	Peaceful; community or species tank	Mid and lower levels	Schooling
Bloodfin	Very active	Peaceful	Mid and upper levels	Schooling; need a lot of space

FISH	Activity Level	Compatibility	Usual Tank Level	Characteristics/ Special Needs
Piranha	Usually quiet	Predatory; adults should be kept with own species	All levels	Schooling; shy; often frightened

CICHLIDS (large, very diverse family)

ASIAN CICHLIDS

Orange Chromide	Moderate; dig pits when breeding	Community tank with other mid-sized fish; aggressive when breeding	Mid and lower	Shy; need retreats

AFRICAN CICHLIDS

African Lake Cichlids (Fuelleborn's Golden, Julies, Malawi Golden, Red-finned, Zebra)	Active; will tear plants	Territorial, quarrelsome, especially when breeding; species tank	All levels; lower	Shy; need plenty of rocky cover; pairs; many are mouthbreeders

Others

Golden-eyed Dwarf	Quiet	Community tank, but aggressive when breeding	Lower	Need shelter

FISH	Activity Level	Compatibility	Usual Tank Level	Characteristics/ Special Needs
Kribensis (Dwarf rainbow)	Quiet	Peaceful; community tank	All levels	Need shelter, hiding places

CENTRAL AMERICAN AND TEXAS CICHLIDS

FISH	Activity Level	Compatibility	Usual Tank Level	Characteristics/ Special Needs
Convict (Zebra)	Moderately active; tear plants	Very aggressive; species tank	All levels	Pairs
Firemouth	Moderately active; may dig and uproot plants	Fairly peaceful with similar-sized fish; species tank preferable	Mid and lower levels	Pairs
Jack Dempsey	Excitable; tear plants	Very pugnacious and territorial; species tank	All levels	Large tank; schools when young, pairs later
Rainbow	Very active	Very compatible with other fish	All levels	Pairs

SOUTH AMERICAN CICHLIDS

FISH	Activity Level	Compatibility	Usual Tank Level	Characteristics/ Special Needs
Angelfish	Slow-moving	Peaceful; can be kept in a community tank with same-sized fish; but better off in species tank	All levels, mostly mid	School, or pair; shy, but may become tame

FISH	Activity Level	Compatibility	Usual Tank Level	Characteristics/ Special Needs
Discus (Pompadour)	Slow-moving	Peaceful, but very territorial and aggressive during breeding; species tank	All levels	Lots of space/hiding places; schools when young, then pairs
Dwarf Cichlids (Agassiz's, Golden-eyed, Ram or Butterfly, Ramiriz')	Moderately active	Generally peaceful, except when spawning, community tank with same-sized fish	Different levels	Hiding places; school when young, then pairs
Festive Cichlid and Flag Cichlid	Moderately active	Quiet, non-aggressive with similar-sized fish; community tank	All levels; mid-water feeder	Pairs; shy at first; may become tame
Oscar (Velvet)	Slow-moving	Species tank, or only with other very strong fish	All levels	Need a lot of space— very large tank; often become hand tame

FISH	Activity Level	Compati- bility	Usual Tank Level	Charac- teristics/ Special Needs

CYPRINIDS (large family, from Europe, Asia, Africa, and North America)

FISH	Activity Level	Compati- bility	Usual Tank Level	Charac- teristics/ Special Needs
Barbs (Black Ruby, Cherry, Clown, Rosy, Tiger)	Very active	Peaceful; community tank with other peace- ful, same- sized fish; tigers may nip other fish's fins	Mid to lower levels	Lots of space/ surface area; schooling; need com- pany
Danios (Giant, Leopard, Pearl, Ze- bra)	Swift, ac- tive, always moving	Nonaggres- sive, good mixers	Upper and mid levels; may leap	Schooling; not scary
Labeos (Red-tailed Black Shark, Red- fin Shark)	Moderately active; play- ful; turns upside- down	Territorial toward own kind; all right with others	Mid to lower swimmer; bottom- feeder	Like hiding places; need plants; can be kept alone
Rasboras (Many sizes and shapes: Harlequin, Red-tailed, Scissor- tailed)	Very active	Peaceful; good in community tank	Upper and mid levels	Schooling; need plants, plenty of room to swim

KILLIFISH (Also called egg-laying toothcarps and top minnows; Af- rica, Asia, North and South America)

FISH	Activity Level	Compati- bility	Usual Tank Level	Charac- teristics/ Special Needs
American Flagfish	Slow- moving, but active dur- ing breed- ing	Aggressive/ pugnacious; species tank	All levels	Algae, plants

FISH	Activity Level	Compati-bility	Usual Tank Level	Charac-teristics/ Special Needs
Lyretails	Active; darts, then rests in water	Species tank	Upper/ surface	Schools, or large groups— more males than fe-males; shaded light; float-ing plants
Panchax(s) (Blue, Cey-lon, Dwarf, Golden, Playfairs)	Lively	Generally peaceful; may be kept with larger fish; preda-tory to smaller fish	Just below water sur-face; good jumper	Schools; lots of floating plants; light/shade
Rachow's Killifish	Slow, but active dur-ing breed-ing	Aggressive with other males; spe-cies tank	Upper and mid levels	Strong light; float-ing plants

LIVEBEARERS (Far East and Central America)

FISH	Activity Level	Compati-bility	Usual Tank Level	Charac-teristics/ Special Needs
Guppies Many vari-eties	Very active	Community tank; com-patible with other fish; males may be quarrel-some with each other	All levels	Schooling; plants; bright light
Halfbeaks	Quiet; rest and then dart	Species tank; males aggressive with each other	Upper level; surface-feeder	Floating plants; schooling

Appendix A

FISH	Activity Level	Compati-bility	Usual Tank Level	Characteristics/ Special Needs
Mollies (Black, Sailfin, etc.)	Active, lively	Community tank; species preferable	All levels; surface-feeder	Schooling; need space, good light, plants, algae
Mosquito Fish (Silver Gambusia)	Lively	Species tank; aggressive, nips other fish's fins	All levels	Schooling; need plenty of space; plants
Platys Many varieties and colors	Lively	Peaceful; community tank	All levels	Schooling; need good light, plants, algae
Swordtails Platy family: many varieties	Active	Peaceful; community tank, large males may be aggressive	All levels; jumper	Schooling; need good light, plants, ample space

LOACHES (Asia, Eurasia)

FISH	Activity Level	Compati-bility	Usual Tank Level	Characteristics/ Special Needs
Clown Loach or **Tiger Botia**	Fast-swimming; basically nocturnal, but may be active during day	Community tank with other peaceful schooling fish	Lower levels; sometimes mid	Schooling; gregarious; need companionship; need soft sand, plants, and hiding places

FISH	Activity Level	Compati-bility	Usual Tank Level	Charac-teristics/ Special Needs
Coolie Loach	Fast-swimming; very active	Nonaggres-sive; com-munity or species tank	Lower lev-els	Nocturnal; need soft sand, plants, hiding-places
Chain Loach or **Dwarf Loach**	Fast-swimming; very active, but will rest on a suface	Species tank, or community tank with similar-sized fish	Mid and lower levels	Best kept in a group; need hiding-places and resting sur-faces

Appendix B

For More Information about Fish Keeping

There are several magazines devoted to keeping fish, all of which contain information on freshwater and marine fish and aquarium and fish-keeping societies. For information write:

Aquarium Fish Magazine
Subscription Department
P.O. Box 484
Mt. Morris, IL 61054-0484
(Published bimonthly)

Freshwater and Marine Aquarium
P.O. Box 487
Sierra Madre, CA 91024
(Published monthly. There is an updated list of specialty societies in each issue.)

Tropical Fish Hobbyist
T.F.H. Publications, Inc.
One TFH Plaza
Neptune City, NJ 07753

Appendix B

Two booksellers that specialize in fishkeeping are:

Lewis Books
P.O. Box 41137
Cincinnati, OH 45241

The Aquatic Book Shop
P.O. Box 276484
Sacramento, CA 95827-6484

If you have a computer and modem, you can subscribe to *Fishnet*, in which aquarium professionals and hobbyists join the Aquaria and Tropical Fish Forum to talk "fish" and exchange information on products, diseases, and news. A voice line is also available. Call CompuServ at (800) 848-8199 to find out how to subscribe.

Glossary of Terms and a Few Pronunciations

Algae: primitive, one-celled aquatic plants that usually contain cholorophyll

Anabantids: pronounced ana-bán-tids

Barbels: whiskerlike "feelers" attached to the mouths of some fish

Brackish: slightly salty

Carnivorous: flesh (meat)-eating

Cichlid: pronounced síck-lid

Community tank: tank, or aquarium, containing more than one kind of fish

Cyprinid: pronounced síp-rin-id

Crustacean: class of predominantly aquatic animals with hard shells and paired, jointed limbs

Detritus: disintegrated matter and debris

Diurnal: active during daylight hours

Ecosystem: an ecological unit of a community of living plants and animals and their environment

Fry: just-hatched fish

Glossary

Invertebrate: an animal without a spine

Loach: pronounced lówch

Mollusk: a marine invertebrate, usually having a shell, such as a clam or snail

Nocturnal: active at night

Omnivorous: eating both meat and vegetable foods

Osmosis: the diffusion of liquid through a semipermeable membrane until there is an equal concentration of fluid on either side of the membrane

pH: a measure of the concentration of hydrogen ions in a solution, and therefore of its acidity or alkalinity. A pH of 7.0 is neutral; below 7 indicates acidity; above 7 indicates alkalinity

Reverse osmosis: a process in which liquid is forced through a semipermeable membrane which filters out dissolved substances and salts

Shoaling: action of swimming together in schools

Spawning: breeding/laying eggs

Species-tank: tank, or aquarium, containing only one kind of fish

Substrate: the gravel or other material covering the bottom of an aquarium

Symbiosis: the close relationship of two or more different individuals, usually beneficial to each

TDS: total dissolved solids—the amount of dissolved substances in water, such as minerals

Toxic: poisonous

About the Author

Elizabeth Randolph writes a regular column for *Family Circle* magazine called "Pets & Wildlife," and is the author of numerous books and articles about pets and pet health. She lives with her husband in Mamaroneck, NY.

About the Consultants

Daniel F. Bebak is Curator of the Mote Marine Science Aquarium on City Island in Sarasota, Florida, which is operated by the Mote Marine Laboratory.

Dr. Paul V. Loiselle is the Assistant Curator of Freshwater Fishes at the New York Aquarium. He has written several books on various aspects of fish keeping and is a contributing columnist to *Aquarium Fish* magazine. He is a former fisheries biologist for the Peace Corps in West Africa.

Brian Morris of Clearwater, Florida, is an expert on breeding and raising discus fish.

Ken Strassfield has been the owner of "Pets Ahoy," a retail establishment in Norwalk, Connecticut, for many years.

Michael K. Stoskopf, DVM, PhD, is Professor and Head of Companion Animal and Special Species Medicine at the College of Veterinary Medicine, North Carolina State University, Raleigh, North Carolina. He is formerly Chief of Medicine at the National Aquarium in Baltimore, Maryland, and Associate Professor of Comparative Medicine and Radiology at Johns Hopkins School of Medicine.

Finally Fawcett has the purrr-fect Pet Care Books